Run Before You Walk

5 Techniques for Start-up Success

Chinmai Swamy

SMART analysis

Published by The Unique SMART Analysis™

First edition

The Unique SMART Analysis™

First published in 2013

Copyright © 2013 Chinmai Swamy

The right of Chinmai Swamy to be identified as the author of this work has been asserted in accordance with sections 77 and 78 of the Copyright Designs and Patents Act 1988

ISBN – 978-0-9575629-0-5

Cover design by Michel Meziane

Book edited by John Harten

www.chinmaiswamy.com

www.runbeforeyouwalkbook.com

www.thesmartanalysis.com

www.ismallbusinessbranding.com

Disclaimer

The author asserts that he cannot be held liable or responsible for the outcomes of decisions the reader makes as a result of reading this book. The reader is wholly responsible for their actions and should seek relevant professional advice before making a decision that may affect their business and life.

The Unique SMART Analysis™

To my family

My lovely wife, Rashmi, without whom I would be a lost ship.

My loving mom, dad and brother who have always inspired me to achieve.

My loving in-laws for their blessings and support.

My grandparents for their love and well-wishes.

My friends, Avinash, Aravind, Aditya, Chetan, Digvijay, Malvika, Roshan, Shilpa and Sharada for supporting me with high spirits and laughter.

I dedicate this book to all the brave entrepreneurs who chase their dreams and make the world a better place.

Foreword

We are living in a fascinating era of entrepreneurs. In the US alone, there were over half million new registered small businesses in 2012. These are exciting times for all of us.

Sadly, statistics show that 90% of them fail to make it into their 3rd year and beyond. One of the main reasons for this sad end to so many small businesses is lack of focus; they forget the basic fundamentals of business and the true spirit of entrepreneurship.

Chinmai has very effectively put together a new meaning for an old, overused acronym SMART™ and addresses the above reasons. Easy to remember but powerful when implemented.

The unique SMART Analysis™ talks about the importance of being customer-focused and providing quality services, highlights the necessity of being agile, discusses beautiful and inspiring new ways on building a great team and company and shows new ways to effectively manage time by talking about delegation and outsourcing.

Raymond Aaron – *New York Times* Best Selling Author
Branding Small Businesses for Dummies

www.aaron.com

Book at a glance

Acknowledgements

Huge thanks to Raymond Aaron, for his inspiring words and powerful questions that provoked me to come out of my comfort zone.

To Lori Murphy, for her timely guidance.

To my school teachers, my Renshi from the Karate dojo and rowing coaches for igniting my passion for excellence and teaching me the importance of a focused life.

To Chris Couldridge for supporting me in this journey.

To my editor, John Harten: I am ever grateful for his professionalism and the clarity he brought to this book. He worked even when he fell ill to meet my impractical deadlines and made it happen.

To my extended family in the UK with whom I have shared eight wonderful years.

To Brijesh Kuttan, for his excellent support and advice in helping build the website for The Unique SMART Analysis™.

To Roshan Pai, for his valuable advice and entrepreneurial guidance.

To Avinash Neal Daniel, for his never ending support, guidance and motivation.

To Rashmi, my lovely and beautiful wife, my friend, my partner in crime, who has supported me all my life, encouraged me during my darkest hours and for making my soul sing every day of my life.

Run

Before

You Walk

The Unique SMART Analysis™

Contents

The Unique SMART Analysis™

The Unique SMART Analysis™

Introduction

Run Before You Walk

"Run before you walk" is a metaphor that means you have the potential to achieve incredible success whether you already own a small business or are thinking of starting one. If you are struggling to find new clients or unable to deliver high quality services to your existing clients to gain more business, you're just walking and not making any successful strides in your business ventures. You have the potential to increase your business, run towards more growth, acquire more clients, and gain more profits.

Run Before You Walk is specifically targeted towards three types of people:

- Entrepreneurs who are thinking of starting a business
- Start-ups that are less than a year old and want to grow bigger (and to run)
- Small businesses established in the last 2-3 years that want to increase in size and expand into the zone of 7-figure revenues

This book delivers the key solutions to all your business problems, provides you with tricks to overcome your day-to-day challenges and gives you the techniques which will enable you to take longer strides in business and achieve success similar to Google, Apple, Samsung, Microsoft, Facebook and Twitter. Yes, like the Silicon Valley giants. You can be the next one.

1

Start taking long strides in business by addressing the five fundamental aspects of your business with simple SMART™ techniques to guide you along the way.

Run your business from day one before getting established.

The reason I decided to write this book was that there are plenty of start-ups and small businesses in the market and each one of you looks similar to the others. This will not work. It is not good for you and, more importantly, it is not good for the customer. Your customer is more frustrated than you because they want to give you business, but they are unable to do that because you are hard to find. It is really hard for them to choose, and in most cases they are not aware of what solutions or services they require that will enable them to solve the problem at hand. *They* are lost in the sea of start-ups and small businesses in the same way *you* are lost in the sea of start-ups and small businesses.

This book is guided by the concept of the new Unique SMART Analysis™.

I already know one SMART and that is for goal setting, so what is this new SMART™? What is this Unique SMART Analysis™?

Well, SMART™ is simple and easy to remember. As an entrepreneur myself I wanted to bring my micro-niche into what already existed in the industry and change it.

2

```
                    Service

          Time                  Market



              Reward       Agility
```

The Unique SMART Analysis™

S – Provide quality SERVICES to your existing clients and increase your brand.

M – Choose your MARKET. Not everybody is your client. Use your micro-niche to add value to your products and services.

A – Have AGILITY in your business; adapt quickly to new trends in your existing customers and look out for new trends in the industry. Don't be complacent.

R – REWARD your team with an opportunity to grow, drive them with a vision and inspire them to be leaders. Be a RESPONSIBLE entrepreneur and support a charity.

T – Devote your TIME only to the important aspects of your business and delegate the rest, outsource and grow.

The Unique SMART Analysis™ will help you build an established brand, grow into a multinational organisation and

3

stand out as a responsible business. The Unique SMART Analysis™ shows that even start-ups like you can take longer strides in business from day one. The longer strides—learning to run—are based on the five aspects of running your business. Most importantly, the word SMART™ highly correlates with today's entrepreneur who is focused and intelligent and who comes up with incredibly simple yet revolutionary concepts and changes the way everyone sees and uses things which were already present.

Entrepreneur of the Day

Today's entrepreneurs believe that they are going to change the world, introduce a new industry and become rich.

I believe there are two types of entrepreneurs:

- Ingredient entrepreneurs
- Recipe entrepreneurs

Ingredient entrepreneurs are the ones who look to make something new out of nothing. They will build a new product or introduce a new service to fill a gap in the market.

Recipe entrepreneurs take what is already there and make something new out of it.

Both kinds of entrepreneurs succeed. We have seen this happen. Apple is a recipe entrepreneur company. They took what was already there, added a micro niche, then packaged and launched the product again back into the market. Henry Ford was an ingredient entrepreneur who introduced automobiles when horses were the primary mode of individual transport. He was persistent and confident in introducing a

4

new kind of engine and he revolutionised the way people travel.

The world needs both types of entrepreneurs. Whichever entrepreneur you choose to become, you will succeed.

We would all enjoy our lives more if we could live it the way we want. We always want to do the activities that enrich us and make us feel we are living our dreams. This can be difficult if you are working for a company. When you work in a job, you are living another person's dream, not your own. You could say it is your dream job, but in fact it is not. You are not allowed to take holidays when you need and when you desire, and you still have to go to work when your mind and soul is partying in Ibiza. You are working towards somebody else's dream.

Would it not be nice if you could be your own boss, decide your own pay, benefits and holidays? Or to decide what work you want to do today and who you want to meet and choose the type of clients you would like to serve? These are the benefits of being an entrepreneur.

Every one of us is an entrepreneur, but the way in which we discover that entrepreneurship is different. Entrepreneurs are made in three ways.

Three Paths to Entrepreneurship

Born Free

Entrepreneurs in this category are born free and wild. They know they can do business and live their life free. Since childhood, they have groomed themselves to be become better leaders, enjoy meeting new people and are good at managing

5

money. They are good at deciding for themselves and have made a lot of mistakes and learned plenty of lessons. They are not shy to ask. Even if they know the answer is going to be a no, they go ahead and try it anyway.

Surprised One

Entrepreneurs in this group are people who have all their life have been led to believe by others, "You need an MBA from Harvard to start a business" and that running a company is too complex and time consuming. This inner attitude has stopped them from reaching their true potential. Having said that, all their life they have always been comfortable with handling pressure and are very calculated in measuring risks; they are extremely passionate about life and want more from it. It is only their mind-set and attitude towards business that is holding them back. It only takes a special moment of self-realisation, an able mentor to guide them or an extra push to overcome their mental block. When they break away from their inner bonds, they realise how simple and practical it is to be a free-spirited entrepreneur.

Pushed and Cornered Entrepreneurs

These entrepreneurs respond to new situations and sudden changes in their perfect lives and rise to the top of the situation in hand. It could be losing a job or a sudden necessity in their personal life. In recent economic times, there have been plenty of sad stories of people being made redundant. It is not a good position to be in when you are made redundant, I know. It happened to me. The initial shock was brutal. But I am so glad it happened because that experience of uncertainty has given me the courage and wisdom to overcome the obstacles in my life and to achieve whatever I set my mind to.

6

"The quality of your life is in direct proportion to the amount of uncertainty you can comfortably live with." – Peter Sage[1].

It's a Hurdle Race

In today's world, not enough entrepreneurs and small businesses are focusing on providing great and quality service to their clients and too often focus on profits and money.

The biggest and the most common challenge faced by today's entrepreneurs, small businesses and start-ups is competition in the market. They worry about the economy. They worry if the next new technology can make their product or service obsolete.

90% of start-ups fail in the first two years. The reasons can vary, but I would like to highlight a few of them now:

- Lack of focus
- Believing that their product/service will serve everyone
- No plan or strategy
- Failing to adapt to and adopt new technologies
- Failing to absorb and implement feedback from clients and customers
- Not having a great team
- Compromising quality for cost-cutting
- Failing to expand and think globally
- Leading an unmotivated team
- Unable to deliver on time

---

[1] Peter Sage is a self-made entrepreneur, speaker and an author. He is currently working on an ambitious space energy project.

The Unique SMART Analysis™

- Unable to spend time and engage with employees and team members
- Aiming to do everything themselves
- Outsourcing the wrong way
- Over-thinking problems and not willing to take action and implement solutions
- Being complacent and not embracing change
- Being too optimistic and expecting great success overnight

The 3G World *of* an Entrepreneur

Every serious entrepreneur has three main goals after getting into business:

- Change the world
- Build a great company and brand
- Earn lots of money

You need to tackle the right goal first to achieve all three goals.

If you go after money first, you risk failing because you will very easily lose track of building a great company and changing the world because you do not have the right team to support your cause.
If you go after changing the world first, you risk failing because you do not have the right team to support your cause all the way; hence you will also not earn lots of money.

The key is to have a great vision and a great team who believes in that vision.

8

Who should read this book?

This book is aimed at three kinds of people.

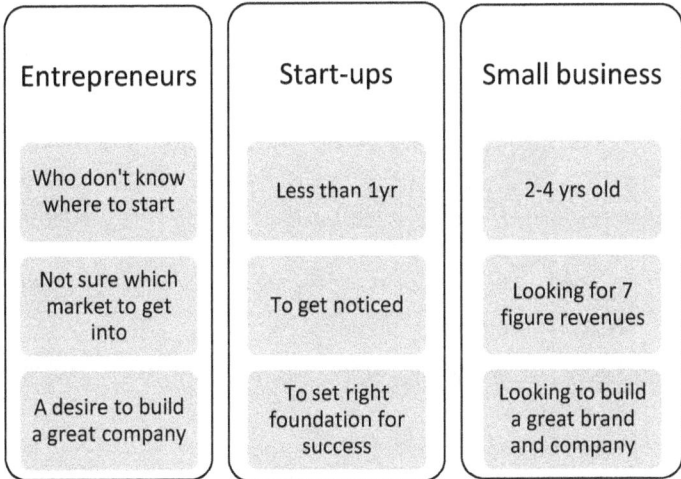

Entrepreneurs	Start-ups	Small business
Who don't know where to start	Less than 1yr	2-4 yrs old
Not sure which market to get into	To get noticed	Looking for 7 figure revenues
A desire to build a great company	To set right foundation for success	Looking to build a great brand and company

Who should read this book?

The budding entrepreneur who is thinking of starting up a company and who doesn't know where to start: they have an idea they believe is new and implementable in the market, one that can earn money.

CEOs and founders of start-ups who are less than a year into their business: this book highlights the common problems and challenges faced by start-ups and provide techniques to overcome these challenges.

This book addresses problems such as:

- Marketing (you're having trouble getting it right)
- No one is noticing you in the market

- People are not buying your services and products
- Time and resource management has left you unproductive
- Cash flow problems have stopped your growth

The CEOs, directors and managers working in small businesses will also be benefitted by reading this book. This book highlights the basic aspects of business which you can incorporate into your everyday work to grow your business and evolve into a great brand. I believe some of the common challenges faced by a small business in today's economic climate are:

- Worried about competition
- Unable to grow because your current plans are not working
- Team and employees are not motivated
- Nobody understands your mission statement
- Not able to increase the value of your brand
- Tried outsourcing and it has not worked to your benefit

The Unique SMART Analysis™ techniques are unique and yet so simple that any of the readers fitting into the above descriptions can start implementing them from day one and can start taking longer strides in their businesses. You'll read more about SMART™ in the next chapter.

How to Use this Book?

Run Before You Walk is your complete guide for achieving:

- An increase in sales
- Getting more clients and getting noticed in the industry
- Branding yourself as an industry expert
- Solidifying your presence in your market niche
- Building a great team and a fantastic company to work for
- Time and resource management
- Marketing strategies
- Success in an ever-changing market

The book talks to three kinds of readers: the budding entrepreneur, new start-ups and existing small businesses. To aid this conversation, chapters are grouped in the same way. Under each group, you will find a list of common challenges. If you want to address any of these challenges, you simply go straight to that chapter. In each chapter, you will find all the relevant topics. However, I would recommend reading all chapters.

I have tried to keep the book simple and practical. If you do not have much time to go through tens of pages then start applying the techniques immediately by jumping straight to *Time To Take Action* chapter. This book is different from other books on the market. It is a reference book that should be in every entrepreneur's pocket, and the size of the book is designed to achieve that.

11

Chapter 1

Who Is a SMART™ Entrepreneur?

Why SMART™ and How It Was Born

In recent times, there has been a tremendous increase in entrepreneurs and small businesses thanks to technology and market growth: anybody and everybody can now set up a company.

In my professional life, I have worked with companies ranging from start-ups to established industry giants. The common trend in these companies was that they were always trying to get clients and they were struggling to meet their targets. Every email sent out by the CEO was all about numbers and sales targets.

As a company grows, it inherits the curse of complacency. It stops adapting to new trends in the market; it stops searching for trends within its own existing client database. Amidst initial success and growing too rapidly, the fundamental aspects of business are often forgotten. This is a slippery slope because once a business starts missing their targets consistently and profits plummet each quarter, companies look towards the only option they have – cutting costs.

Some of the common ways small businesses cut costs:

- Redundancy
- Reduce the number of processes
- Reduce budget for growth
- Overwork existing staff
- Stop training programs for staff

These measures to cut costs come at a price: the quality of your SERVICES is compromised. You fail to notice emerging client trends and ignore the importance of ADAPTING. As a company, you will start to measure all operations of your business in only two units:

1. Time
2. Money

You forget to address the important aspects of entrepreneurship like:

- Encouraging growth of your employees
- Engaging with your team
- Innovating new products and services
- Providing an emotional experience to your existing clients

Instead of focusing on your existing clients, you start channelling your resources towards marketing to gain new clients.

Another problem I noticed is that in each company, everybody seemed to be very busy, especially the founder, CEO and the board of directors. They were always attending meetings, chasing deadlines and targets, preparing for meetings, preparing for demos, or working on projects. With all this, they forgot to engage with their team. They forgot to encourage growth and they stopped building leaders.

As an entrepreneur, if your reason and passion for doing business is as great as your service, you will always be in business because people will always come to you.

The Unique SMART Analysis™

The Unique SMART Analysis™ is about the five fundamental aspects of doing business: services, market niche, agility, rewarding your team and time. SMART™ highlights the importance of each the five aspects and also provides you with a blueprint for success when approaching your business.

Providing Quality SERVICES

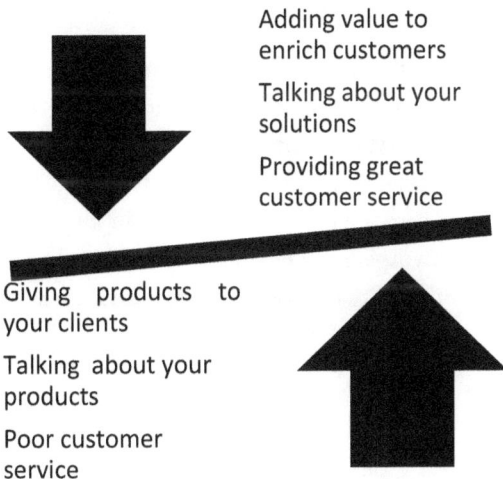

Adding value to enrich customers

Talking about your solutions

Providing great customer service

Giving products to your clients

Talking about your products

Poor customer service

Providing quality SERVICES

15

In the budding entrepreneur chapter, techniques on service are focused on refining your thoughts about your start-up when you are grooming yourself to be an entrepreneur, when you are shaping your ideas and when polishing your product. Quality is driven by your motivation, and your motivation is to solve your end-users' problems. This book will provide you with the techniques and mindset that help you think about, plan and manage your product from the earliest stage, embedding the concept of service and quality and enrichment.

The chapter on start-ups highlights the importance of having a feedback loop with your customers to measure yourself and improve the quality of your service. During the first year of a start-up, it is very easy to get busy and lose focus on your intended service and quality. It is the time where, as a start-up, you are more focused on getting more clients, getting more leads, networking and developing your brand. You are so busy doing more than one task that it is very easy to lose track of who you initially set out to serve.

Once you survive the initial eighteen months of start-up, your priorities will change. You will come to several crossroads where your core values of service and quality will be questioned and challenged. This book is an action guide for you which you can refer to at any point in the life of your business so that you are never on the road that forces you to trade service and quality for cost, resources and time.

MARKET Niche

Be yourself; everyone else is already taken. – Oscar Wilde[2]

Last year alone, the US registered close to half a million small businesses. Obviously, adding numbers from the United Kingdom, Europe, India, Brazil, Africa and China would increase that number quite a bit. This is a big issue for the end-user. Customers enjoy giving their business to the right product or service provider. Even before they find a provider, they are forced to go through a frustrating journey to identify the right one for them. The sheer number of choices available makes finding the right business very difficult. It is critical that you make your business stand out.

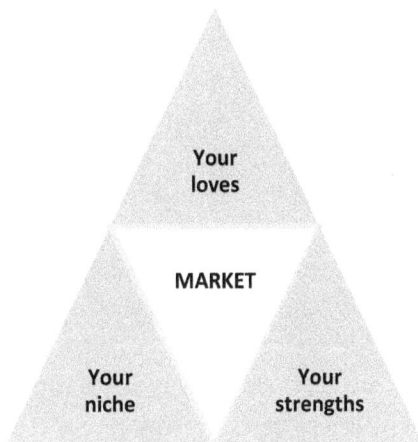

MARKET and your niche

Most businesses want to do the same things that have already been done.

---

[2] Oscar Wilde – Irish writer and poet

17

If you're part of a herd, your view will always be the same - Raymond Aaron[3]

As a budding entrepreneur, as a start-up or as the owner of an established business, it is very important for you to make sure you don't get lost in the sea of sameness. You have to establish a brand and identity around your service and product and establish yourself as an industry expert by choosing a single market niche. If you go after everybody, you're not going after anybody. You need to target your audience by packaging your services and products for a particular type of customer. You will be able to do that in a better way once you focus your energy in one industry and in one market and address only one particular type of client.

As an example, if a gardener would like to grow his business by adopting new technology or partnering with another gardener across the world, he might search for IT solutions for his technology needs. As an IT solutions company, you can then build a website so that he can increase sales, improve his customers' interaction and relationship with his business, and maintain an inventory of his stock. You will be able to think of all possible solutions for your gardener client if you have positioned yourself as THE IT solutions provider for gardeners. You are now an industry expert in providing IT solutions to gardeners all over the world.

AGILITY in Your Process

Agility is the capability of a company to rapidly adapt to the changing market and other environmental shifts and be more

---

[3] Raymond Aaron is a great mentor, speaker and a *New York Times* bestselling author. I am lucky to have him as my mentor.

productive and maintain cost-effective ways of delivering quality and service to the client despite those changes.

The difference between being in business after three years or even after six months is having the agility, the adaptability and the flexibility to gather information, analyse it, change and move forward. As you have seen, the big corporations really suffer in being able to incorporate this fundamental important aspect of business. Consider HMV, Jessops and Blockbuster: these companies are only the most recent victims of not being agile and have gone into administration. They failed to adapt to recent changes in their industries. They failed to recognise that people are getting used to the concept of accessing their content online. They stuck to the conventional methods of sales by selling products in-store. They failed to recognise the importance of online accessible entertainment media such as iTunes, Google Play and Spotify, and due to this one mistake they are into administration.

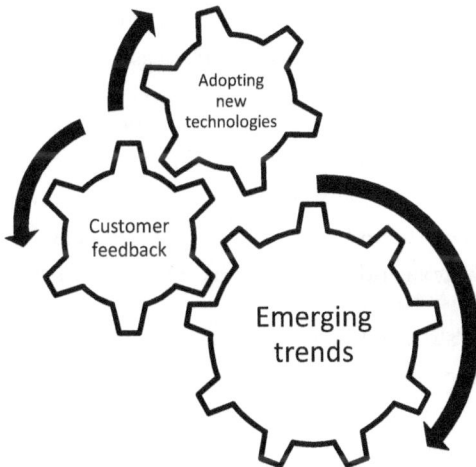

AGILITY in your process

19

Agility is also about having different options for different clients.

Different clients have different requirements, and every one of them has to be served with the same quality and value. If you are working from a model of one single process, then to achieve quality across different types of clients will be difficult.

- Do you have agility in your operations to cater to different trends in your market?
- Do you have the attitude to adapt to the latest trends in your market?

REWARD Your Team

As an entrepreneur, you have great aspirations and you have a vision of what you want your company to grow into. In this process, you will need people to help you get there. You need the right people on your journey and they should be ready to help you and understand your business. They must share your vision and contribute towards your success. To achieve this, you have to have a reward system to attract the right people.

If money is your only target, you will find it harder to get more of it because you can never directly go after money and success. One of the most efficient, prudent, proven blueprints to achieve success is to have a vision, one powered by an objective goal and fuelled by passionate people behind it.

In today's current economic climate, everyone who is working for a company or small business is driven by money. This is not good. Imagine you have hired a talented employee, giving him an excellent pay package or that you have involved a new partner by offering a share of the company. When there is a

20

change in that person's economic situation, then the initial passion to work for the company starts to evaporate. That passion then only lasts for no more than six months. This is a common problem in all kinds of industries and all sizes of business.

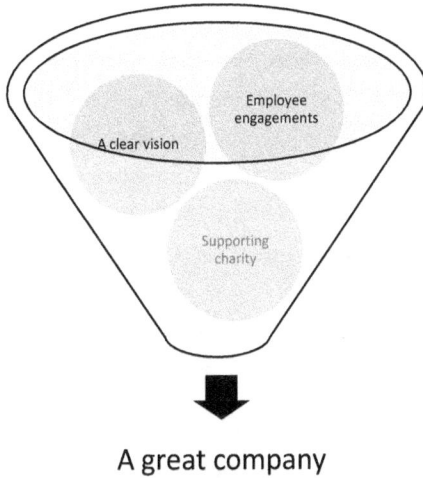

A great company

REWARD your team

You need to REWARD your team with:

- Opportunities to grow
- Opportunities to become leaders within your organisation
- You need to give them a vision that resonates with their souls

To get the most out of your employees or your partners, you need to give them more than just a number to make them

21

passionate. They need a goal and a belief that what they are doing is important. If your employees believe in the company's goals, they will be more committed. A company vision and stated goals will help you to engage your employees, will help attract investment in your company, and will help attract customers.

One of the most common problems faced by entrepreneurs like you is having the right people who can understand the business and who can and will operate on their own even if you are not in it. It takes a tremendous amount of time and trust to let your partner or your team member handle a client on their own without you chairing or being in the meeting ensuring things are done properly. Don't be held back by your own inhibitions, fears and doubts. If you have the right team, you will know they share the vision and values of your company.

In today's world, you have to lead by example. You have to reward, recognise and support your society by giving back. Every enterprise must support a charity, support their society and be responsible about the resources they consume. These attributes will propel your brand into a global one.

Reward is empowering your employees and team to become the leaders your enterprise needs.

Reward is being responsible to your society by supporting a charity, or perhaps by helping young college graduates by providing internships.

TIME

Time is money and this timeless adage has become one of the most translated proverbs across the world.

Delivering on time to your customers is critical. It builds trust and a long-term relationship. To achieve timeliness and maintain quality, each time, for every different client, may seem like a challenge. But it is only a challenge if you believe it is.

This is easily achieved by choosing any of these techniques:

- Outsourcing
- Delegation
- Partnering
- Collaborating

These options can be implemented at the level best suited for you. Tasks can be delegated to a friend from college or to an outsource unit in India.

Things you must do

Things you wish to do

Things you like to do

TIME and tasks

23

Taking time off your business to enjoy life and cherish your soul is critical. This is possible only if you are outside of your business. Only when you are outside of your business can you spot vital aspects within it. You will be more focused towards growth and strategically better placed to steer your business in the sea of business and succeed. You will be able to easily implement growth strategies. There will be more time for you to network and build relationships with potential partners or venture capitalists and get more involved in enhancing your brand and the value of your company.

The Unique SMART Analysis™ will help you plan, implement and maintain the success of your business. Staying focused on service, agility, market niche, rewards and time will allow you to concentrate your efforts on building long-term relationships with your customers and growing your business rather that constantly chasing leads.

An end-user might be a hungry customer waiting in a restaurant for his food. The common element here is time, and it so often happens that service providers position themselves to fail on product delivery because they want to do everything on their own without considering the benefits of delegation, contracting and outsourcing.

Chapter 2

Why Do You Need to Be SMART™?

The Unique SMART Analysis™ techniques will enable you to:

- Increase your revenues
- Increase your profits
- Get more clients
- Attract investments
- Overcome cash flow problems
- Convert your down-time into an incredible uptime
- Get noticed as an industry expert
- Attract the best talent in the market to come and work in your company and stay
- Form an incredible team driven by passion and vision
- Identify your niche in the market
- Become a global business through partnerships and collaborations
- Deliver your product on time by implementing techniques of outsourcing and delegation.

Originally, this book was aimed mainly at technology start-ups and small businesses. When I launched my Facebook fan page about The Unique SMART Analysis™, some of my friends

25

who were entrepreneurs approached me and asked if my techniques could help them too. So I started offering my services to them for free to see if they worked, and they did. This made me remove the word "technology" from the subtitle and just call it "Five Techniques For Start-Up success." SMART Analysis™ can help everybody.

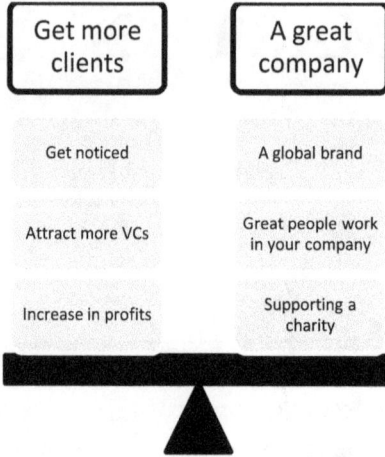

SMART™ benefits

SMART Analysis™ can be applied to situations like the ones below:

You have just finished college and you have plans of setting up your own business or you have unlocked your entrepreneurship side and want to sell your idea. How will you kick-start your start-up such that you will start making money from day one?

You have a new start-up business, and you've just finished the first project and made your first client happy. Now, how can you continue to get more clients and keep the momentum?

26

You have been running your small business with some success. Now you want to catapult your brand to the next level and evolve it into a global brand.

Testimonials from CEOs and business owners

As an entrepreneur myself I urge you to read the book and apply his SMART™ techniques.

Arun Shroff
CEO and Founder of FrontPoint Systems Ltd

Entering the business world is an act of courage and nothing saddens me more but to see how society fails to help entrepreneurs achieving their dreams. I always wonder why so many entrepreneurs are pulling out of the race before they even had a taste of sustainable wealth.

What Chinmai Swamy is giving us is invaluable: the formula to guaranteed success, growth, and profits. 'Run before you walk' is a book of personal discovery; you can access not only the author's wealth of experience as a business analyst but the map to your own bespoke solutions. Reading this book you realise that success is within reach and it is, actually, a personal choice. Regardless of your age or background, learning to 'Run before you walk' is one solution that can successfully apply to any type of business.

I just love Chinmai's concept, because SMART™ is the very fabric of entrepreneurship and should be mandatory for any serious entrepreneur.

Marina Nani
Author of the Double Award Winning
Book Series 'Away from Home'
Founder of The Hotel Alternative™ and S.A.V.E. Trips™

27

As a business owner I would like to say I was so impressed by the Title "Run before you walk", it explains a lot. The concept is put in simple language which helps anybody and everybody who is starting a business.

Chaula Patel
Business owner
Chaulas Indian restaurant
East Sussex, UK

The new SMART™ is a great framework for organisations to analyse their business and position themselves for the next iteration of growth. Use the SMART™ techniques as a lens to identify your business' key strengths and improvement areas and develop a 360 degree view of your organisation.

Neal Daniel
Head of Business transformation
Chubb Insurance, Europe

It takes courage to attempt to redefine a word already in business usage but Chinmai has done this and given a new meaning to the word SMART. Discover his simple yet profound success mind-set template for busy entrepreneurs.

Mike Pitt
Founder & CEO
Marketing Fundamentals Ltd
Author of *How To TurboCharge Your Business With a Blog*

With this book Chinmai has provided a very practical and hands on method of how entrepreneurs can stay on top of their businesses and grow them. The SMART framework will really provide them not just the tools but also the mindset to succeed in their business..

Aravind Krishna
Business Consultant, Vodafone UK

28

Chapter 3

I Have an Idea, but I Don't Know Where to Start

A 10,000 mile journey begins with a single step.

Ideas are worthless. If you have an idea, it's time to action it. An idea should be actionable. Even if it's something others have done, that's okay as long as you are adding an extra element to that idea. You have to be yourself, or, as Oscar Wilde said, "Be yourself because everybody else is taken."

You do not pass an exam to know if you are ready to be an entrepreneur; it is just a feeling you get, one backed up by an inner voice saying, "You need to do this now," or "You are ready now," or "Let's do it and find out."

29

This is a new journey on which you are about to embark. On this journey you are going to have plenty of opportunities disguised as challenges. You will need to push yourself to achieve your success. It is important that you pack two vital items in your bag:

1. Your passion
2. Your loves

Innovation is not a silver bullet, and it won't give you overnight success. It is a window of opportunity for you to implement your innovative idea and improve it as you go along. You must work with this innovative idea to make it better and more efficient so that later you can add more value to the end-user and client, so it can resolve their issues, and so it can connect to your potential clients emotionally.

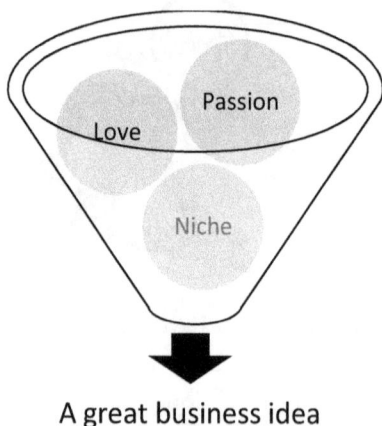

A great business idea

Ingredients for a business idea

This highlights the importance of being unique. You need to bring this authenticity into the business and into your idea. Ideas are worthless unless you implement. You do not have to

30

wait for your idea to be perfect before you implement. You do not have to be the next Facebook, the next Apple or the next Google. You just have to be a new you; on this journey, you're defining a new world around you.

You don't have to be great to start, but you have to start in order to be great. So if you are contemplating and procrastinating, you are not yet great; you haven't achieved your success. So start now, today.

Tomorrow is another day, another start. Let's worry about that tomorrow. Right now, today, you're making a new start.

There's no greater thing that you can do with your life, than to follow your passions in a way that serves you and the world – Sir Richard Branson[4]

What You Really Want

Think what you could achieve with your idea if money (or other challenges) were not an issue. Achieving clarity about your idea is more important than money or other hurdles. Once you have clarity, then you will be able to overcome any hurdle that is laid in front of you.

An idea is born in the presence of a leader. The initial concept for a start-up or a business starts with a leader, and a business' best ideas should be nurtured by its leader. A leader should have perseverance and be willing to listen to potential ideas. A leader should lead the idea, the team and the company even in the darkest times. A leader stands on the deck and watches out for icebergs. A leader steers the ship in the right direction when it is going off course.

---

[4] Sir Richard Branson – Founder and chairman of Virgin Group

---

People buy the passion you put into your idea and product. Be yourself and be passionate about your idea.

You will be able to ride on this new journey seamlessly and effortlessly when your innovative idea or product or service is guided by your vision. It is the vision that will give you clarity on where you have to go and how you will get there.

The most important point is this: do not wait until you have achieved perfection for your service or product. No product can be perfect. A product should serve its purpose of adding value to the customer or client. It should be simple and it should be effective. It should be attractive and deliver emotional satisfaction, and its use should be intuitive.

To Follow or Not to Follow

You don't necessarily have to be the first to be in the market to achieve success. You can also enter the market second or tenth and still achieve success. Perhaps the greatest example is Apple. Apple was not the first to enter into mobile phone devices. Apple was not the first to enter touchscreen smart devices, and Apple was not the first to enter into the market of handheld tablets. But when Apple did enter the market, it had positioned itself as a champion in those products by learning from other competitors who were already in the market. It learnt from the mistakes they made. Apple learnt from the way the user interacted with other products from different competitors in the market. Apple understood the behaviour of the user and Apple delivered. Thus, Apple made an impact and dominated the market when it did arrive in the market

We should also consider the story of Hotmail, and how the founders wanted to design one thing but ended up delivering

32

something different. They encountered a problem in the process of designing their new concept. And when they tried to address that, they came up with Hotmail. If you have a problem in your life and you are not finding services and products that address it, then you can make the solution available for other people like you. You have found your idea, and then you know exactly how it should be implemented, and you know exactly who to target. You will know exactly what type of people they will be, because in some way, they are you. You need to package your service into a product or make the service available and launch it immediately. It may not be perfect at the start, but you can always refine it as you go along. Always be open to refining your ideas and quickly address those enhancements and release them back to the market.

You have to identify your micro-niche. You do not go after everybody, because everybody is not your client. Your services and products will not help everybody in the world. This illusion is one of the main reasons why 90% of start-ups and small businesses fail within the first two years. They fail because they believe that their services and products will help everybody. Your solution must be focused on a very specific type of client.

Be authentic. Your idea, your services or your products must have all the authentic attributes of *you*. Once you can identify what defines you and how you are different from the rest of the world, you will then be able to easily apply your authentic style to your services and products, which will then become unique in the market. Do not pretend to be somebody else, not even your role model. When you have a role model, you apply the skills and behaviour of that person in your life, but you would still do it in your own way. So find your authentic spirit and be yourself.

When you focus on a specific type of client, you will gain the advantage of knowing everything about the client. You will know where to market your services and products, you will know when to market services and products, and you will know what type of packaging to design for your services and products. You will know which geographical location you should focus on more to attract a specific type of client.

Broadcast Your Idea

Now that you have found your idea and added your niche to it, you need to announce it to the world. That's right, you need to get yourself a TV tower and broadcast it on your channel across the world.

How do you do it?

Off-line and online broadcasting

Online Broadcasting

In the world we live in today, there are readily made tools available like:

- Twitter
- Facebook
- Google+
- Pinterest
- YouTube

34

Online broadcasting

You can use the above platforms to share your ideas and get immediate feedback from your friends, family and your potential clients.

Since this is the first iteration of your idea, there are several ways to position yourself online to talk about your new idea and get readers' feedback. You can either spend time and money in building a very expensive website or just launch one by using the free services readily available. I would advise most to use free services because you are still starting and not yet ready to do business.

In the initial days of start-up, you can make use of these channels even when you're still thinking of an idea. You need to have an online presence broadcasting your solutions and connecting emotionally with the reader. You don't have to wait for your service or product to be ready; you do not have to wait for funding; the moment you have found an idea or a product which will satisfy a certain emotional need in the market, you can publish it on-line. Feedback from those who see interact with your online presence will help you to fine tune your idea.

The Unique SMART Analysis™ advocates providing excellent services to your clients and customers. Providing excellent

35

services starts with being clear on what you are going to offer. When you talk about your ideas and products, you will not convey the right message so it is necessary for you to convey an emotion, a solution that will enrich the end-user.

Please do not talk about your product and its uniqueness in the industry; your customer is least concerned with your products. They are more concerned about what you deliver. Your delivery is a solution that adds value. You need to talk about that value, and how you will provide a solution to a problem they have.

More information on this is covered in the chapter *Marketing Is a Bitch*. I would not say at this stage for you to call this endeavour marketing because you are only doing a beta test of your products and services.

Off-line Broadcasting

Now it's time to go and meet people and interact with them in person and test your idea.

Off-line broadcasting

Interact with Local Meetup Groups

Once you have identified your market, it will give you initial clarity on the type of people to target. Using established platforms like Meetup.com find out where your target audience meet and join that Meetup.com group and attend their meetings.

Refining Your Ideas to Become Solutions

Your solution, especially your first one, doesn't have to be perfect. But you have to make it available for your potential clients and end-users to use it. You can refine it as you go along.

I listened to customer's feedback and introduced monthly Friday Curry night. - Chaula[5]

Fail quickly, iterate fast. - Arun Shroff[6]

You can use a survey or a feedback mechanism through your end-users to change it rapidly. There are several technologies and platforms made readily available for you to get valuable feedback from your clients to your doorstep. Please refer to my *Time to Take Action* chapter to see how you can start getting valuable (and often free) feedback instantly.

Free Online Survey Engines

- ☐ MailChimp
- ☐ Survey Monkey
- ☐ Kwik Surveys
- ☐ Dot Surveys
- ☐ Survey Expresion

---

[5] Chaula – Owner of chain of restaurants in East Sussex, UK
[6] Arun Shroff – CEO and founder of FrontPoint Systems

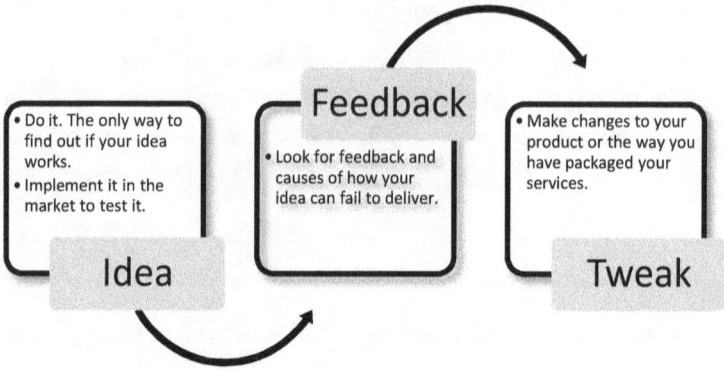

Implementing your ideas

Do not guess: when you guess, you fail. Test your idea immediately.

Funding Your Idea

There are several proven methods of funding your idea. All of them work. It is for you to decide which one will suit your idea better. This funding is for your idea and not for you. I say this because most people overfund their initial start-up and risk spending too much money on stuff they did not need. Similarly, you should not underfund your idea and risk its success.

Funding your idea

Bootstrap Your Idea

Now that you have tested your idea both online and off-line, you will have a sense of what the initial reaction was for your idea. You can bootstrap your idea, which is funding yourself by making use of all your available resources and effectively utilizing them. This is sometimes also called a garage start-up.

Mike Pitt[7], CEO and founder of Marketing Fundamentals, Ltd bootstrapped his business concept by saving money. He worked as contractor initially so that he could save extra to fund his new venture. Once he hit his financial target, he set his idea free and started his new company.

Arun Shroff also bootstrapped his first business after earning his MBA from the Indian Institute of Management, Ahmedabad. He was one of the few graduates who started their own company after university. His first business was started in the early 90's when personal computers were an emerging market in India. He made use of the latest market trend and successfully launched his first enterprise, Dynapro, which repackaged and resold computers for small businesses.

I can go on with this list by talking about Google, Apple, Microsoft and how they started their initial days of start-up by bootstrapping their business.

You do not always need money, but you need a better strategy. – Peter Sage

I was working on a full-time contract to use the money to support the new business. I knew there would come a day when I would be ready to move into my own business. – Mike Pitt

---

[7] Mike Pitt – CEO and founder of Marketing Fundamentals Ltd

39

Let the Public Fund You

Kickstarter is a funding platform for creative projects, every kind of project you can think of: films, games, music, art, design and technology. Kickstarter is full of ambitious, innovative, and imaginative projects that are brought to life through the direct support of others. Since Kickstarter launched, it has facilitated 30,000 creative projects across all domains with over $350 million dollars. This funding was from the public. Over 2.5 million people have funded Kickstarter projects across the world.

With advances made in global collaboration in e-commerce, you can easily get prototypes done in China or India for a fraction of what it would cost in Europe or North America. There is no need to bulk order. (3D printers have done wonders for making one-off prototypes reasonably priced.)

This is truly an inspired generation aspiring towards enriching the planet with new ideas. People like you who can float an idea on a website and test it by sharing the site across the several social platforms.

Let the Angels Fund You

The most famous and proven type of funding is venture capitalist funding. You do not necessarily have to walk into a dragon's den to get your funding. You can find many venture capital meetings in your local area by using Meetup.com groups.

Also, if you can find a company that is closely related to your product or service, then reach out to them and seek out funding. If that company has a like-minded CEO and founder

40

like you, you will have a better chance of getting help from them.

You serve for money, not sell for money

In the early days of being an entrepreneur, you must embed this very important characteristic of a great entrepreneur in the deepest part of your mind.

This is a great quote simply because it highlights two aspects of your business: one, that your business is about serving people and thereby you connect emotionally; and two, you understand your end-user and you want to help them by adding value to their life. These are great characteristics to have as an entrepreneur because when you start your journey with the right motives, you will go a long way on the journey to your success and touch people's hearts and add value to the lives along the way. So don't sell your products for money: you sell your products to add value to other people's lives for money.

The Unique SMART Analysis™ strongly focuses on the concept of addressing your client by adding great quality service. Identify a value or service within you that you can offer to enrich people's lives

Having an idea and passion is only half the work; you need to start putting them in action; however small it might seem - Chaula

The biggest risk is not taking a risk at all – Arun Shroff

Make tweaks and pivot but don't give up, just keep moving. – Mike Pitt

Ideas:

Your passions:

_____

Niches:

_____

Your skills:

_____

Ideal Client:

_____

Online Broadcasting

```
┌─────────────────────────────────────┐
│                                     │
│                                     │
└─────────────────────────────────────┘
```

Off-line Broadcasting

```
┌─────────────────────────────────────┐
│                                     │
│                                     │
└─────────────────────────────────────┘
```

Resources needed

```
┌─────────────────────────────────────┐
│                                     │
│                                     │
└─────────────────────────────────────┘
```

Funding required

```
┌─────────────────────────────────────┐
│                                     │
│                                     │
│                                     │
│                                     │
└─────────────────────────────────────┘
```

The Unique SMART Analysis™

Chapter 4

Going Solo

This chapter is dedicated to the brave-hearted entrepreneurs who are looking to start up their own business. These are exciting and challenging times. If you want to come out on top and get your foot in the door, you need it to start right.

Eagles don't fly with ducks. - Mark Victor Hansen[8]

Clear Your Inner Circle

Show me five people you know and meet regularly; tell me five thoughts you think regularly; tell me five habits you do on a regular basis and I will tell you who you will be and how your business will grow.

If John wants to become an artist, then the most natural and obvious behavioural change John would do is to:

- John would start going to artists' open houses
- John would meet and interact with artists
- John would set up a place in his house to unleash his creativity
- John would start meeting people who are appreciative of art
- John would get more involved in art activities and visit places focused on art to get inspiration

---

[8] Mark Victor Hansen – Founder and co-creator of Chicken Soup for the Soul book series.

- John would read more books related to art and inspiration.
- John would make sure his inner circle of friends is now filled with more artists.

What can we learn from John the artist? Since you are planning to start up your business, you now need to change the way you think, focus your energy, your activities and your friends.

- You need to start going to entrepreneur networking events.
- You need to interact with other entrepreneurs.
- You need to set up a place in your home which will be the first desk of your company.
- You need to read books related to start-ups and entrepreneurs.
- You need to make sure your inner circle of friends is now filled with more entrepreneurs.
- You need to change the bookmarks on your browser so that you read more about start-ups and entrepreneurship.
- You need to follow successful CEOs on your Twitter accounts and add them into your Google+ circles.

Have a Role Model

You should have a role model, a friend or a successful entrepreneur who you admire. The person can be from the field of your business or in the field of your industry or in your own personal life. You need to find out what positive activities that person does on a regular basis. You need to find out what kind of inspirational habits that person passionately and regularly does.

44

Once you have this information, you can then analyse and apply similar trends and behaviour to your own life.

When you recognise and appreciate the qualities and characteristics of your role model, this means that you have the same qualities and characteristics inside you. You need to believe that you are that person and that you have those qualities and skills and characteristics already. You only need to tap into your inner self and break away from the normal routine to which you have become a slave.

Eliminate Negatives

Bad energy in your life will affect and bring bad energy to your business. You need to take time and sort out your personal life and remove any negative emotions and negative behaviour you have inside so that you can become a success in your business. You need to spend time with your inner self, reflect upon the people who you love and increase your positive energy. You need to start doing activities that bring happiness to you and increase the positive energy in your life. The time you spend in these activities can be as little as a moment each day and you will see the returns in your business immediately.

Start with Motivation and Set Your Goals High

Motivation is a champion's breakfast. Start your day with a bit of motivation. Refine your focus before you start any activity each day.

Have a list of items that motivates you and keep it handy. This will be your way of ensuring you stay motivated.

45

Add an activity to your life that will be the first activity you do when you wake up in the morning, regularly. That activity can be:

- Meditation
- Reading and listening to inspirational speakers
- Talking to your coach or mentor

The activity can be as simple as opening the window and showing gratitude for a beautiful day.

Goal Setting

If you know how to reach your current goals, then you have set them too low. The magic of having a goal is to make you come out of your comfort zone and do something different and inspire you to try new things. It is always the case that your goals and your dreams are outside of your comfort zone.

A higher goal will help you discover new qualities within you. If you plan a goal within your comfort zone, then it is not a goal; it is just another activity that will result in an outcome you already know and will not be a greater success, the success you seek to achieve. Aim for the stars, if you fail, you will land on the moon.

Have a Plan

A business plan is essential. A business plan can start off on a sheet of paper and then make its way into a ten-page (or longer) Word document. There are three types of business plan:

1. **Mini plan**

   This plan is your route map for the year.

2. **Working plan**

   A Wikipedia of your company's operational strategy.

3. **Presentation plan**

   An attractive presentation document you will use to attract venture capitalists, bankers and potential clients.

For more information of how to write a business plan and what to include in it, please refer to *Time to Take Action* chapter.

Enrich Your End-User

Once you are satisfied with your idea, now carefully package your product into a service that can enrich the end-user.

Once you have identified your market niche, then establish yourself as an industry expert in that market. This is done very easily.

Answer these questions to find out your business niche:

- Whose lives or businesses are you going to enrich?
- What is the current problem they are facing?
- How can your solution fix the problem?
- What level of customer satisfaction will be experienced by using your service?
- How will you provide the service?
- What will the customer have to do in order to implement the service?
- How many different kinds of clients and customers are you targeting?
- How are they different from one another?

47

Test Your Idea

You have an idea, and that's great. Before you pursue it further, you need find answers to some of the important questions:

- Is this idea unique?
- If unique, which industry or market am I trying to aim for?
- How will this idea enrich the end-user or your customers?
- What kind of client problems is this idea solving?
- Is there another idea similar to mine?
- If there is, how different is mine from theirs?
- If the idea is no different, then what value within me can make a difference?
- Is the current idea in the market applied to only one industry?
- Can I form a synergy or partnership with the current establishment in the market?
- If yes, then will I be able to repackage my idea such that it enriches a particular niche market?

This is how your thought process should be when deriving a concept out of your initial idea.

By doing this, you are going to uncover potential challenges that you may face in the initial days of your business so that you can prepare for them. In this process, you will identity your strengths and weaknesses; you will uncover your "why" and your vision; you will develop a business plan; you will find new partners and a new you.

48

Start Building a Brand

When you have a brand, you set yourself to stand out from the sea of sameness. A client identifies you by your brand. You need to ensure that brand is echoed by everything you and your company does. As the leader and CEO of your brand, you need to live, talk and do whatever your brand is about. You need to be passionate about your brand at any given point of time. Congratulations on your first step as an entrepreneur! You chose to try something new by buying this book and have improved your chances of success from day one.

Remember: the speed limit is only for the safety of motorists driving on roads, not for you and your business. If you feel you have the right idea and a clear vision of what lies ahead, then step on the accelerator and cruise to your maximum potential.

You, don't stop when clock turns 3 AM,

You, don't stop because you are tired,

You, don't stop for other reasons,

You stop when your goal is ACHIEVED.

-Chinmai Swamy

All the best on your new journey!

Friends:

Goals: _____

Role Models: _____

Your skills: _____

Brand: _____

_____

Idea

```
┌──────────────────────────────────┐
│                                  │
│                                  │
│                                  │
└──────────────────────────────────┘
```

Uniqueness of your idea

```
┌──────────────────────────────────┐
│                                  │
│                                  │
│                                  │
└──────────────────────────────────┘
```

Which problem does your idea solve?

```
┌──────────────────────────────────┐
│                                  │
│                                  │
│                                  │
└──────────────────────────────────┘
```

Steps to implement your idea

```
┌──────────────────────────────────┐
│                                  │
│                                  │
│                                  │
│                                  │
│                                  │
│                                  │
└──────────────────────────────────┘
```

The Unique SMART Analysis™

Chapter 5

Partners

As we discussed in an earlier chapter, when you have a brand, you need to ensure that brand is echoed in everything you, your company and your company's team members and employees do. As the leader and CEO of your brand, you need to live, talk and do whatever your brand is about. You need to be passionate about your brand at any given point of time. And if you have a partner or partners, they need to demonstrate the same commitment to the brand.

Finding the Right Partner

You are more likely to survive and succeed in the early days of entrepreneurship if you have a partner. If you look at all the major successful companies in the world, all them had cofounders working together. Apple had Steve jobs and Steve Wozniak. Google had Larry Page and Sergey Brin. Twitter was founded by Evan Williams and Biz Stone. Microsoft had Bill Gates and Paul Allen. Hewlett-Packard had Bill Hewlett and Dave Packard. eBay was founded by Pierre Omidyar and Jeffrey Skoll. Intel was founded by Gordon Moore and Bob Noyce, and Yahoo was founded by Jerry Yang and David Filo.

I'm not saying you can only have two partners to begin a successful business, but trying to do all of it on your own is a hard task. You won't be as successful as you might be if you

51

join up with another partner or two. Find a like-minded partner who can complement your strengths. If you're an engineer, find a great salesperson. If you're a great salesperson, find a great engineer. Diversifying your founding team is the way to go forward. When you have a team of cofounders who have different areas of expertise and perspectives, each of them will add a niche quality, characteristic and attitude to your team, helping the business become a greater success. Don't worry about losing out on profits by sharing them.

It is better to have a little of something big than have a lot of something small. – Raymond Aaron

Starting a business all by yourself can be a huge task and will most certainly take its toll on you. It will easily burn you out. Try to start it with a partner or a team of like-minded people.

Unity is strength.

Each one should come with a niche skill that is important. If all of you want to do the same task, you will have skill redundancy and perhaps conflict. There will be many different tasks that need to be done, and each partner should be able to contribute a different expertise. Tasks that fall in to common categories can be shared.

Start Together, Work Together

Starting with partners has other benefits. The workload is distributed; more people are involved and importantly all the work gets done in little time.

Having friends as your partners can be wonderful. It's good that you have all come together and decided to change your lives, but it's equally important that there are clear agreements

52

in place in order to serve the new company best and to preserve the friendships.

- Find out why each of your partners wants to start the company.

- Find what each person enjoys doing.

- Find out each person's strengths and weaknesses.

- Agree on a common vision for the company.

- Highlight different tasks needed to run the company and distribute responsibilities according to individual tastes and strengths.

- Agree on the division of stock in the company. An equal share for all may not be a good idea. Identify who is doing the most important task in the company and divide the stakes accordingly. It is better to have this discussion at an early stage (when things are running smoothly) rather than when one partner decides to quit.

- Have an easy exit strategy. This is important, because in the initial stages everyone will say, "I am committed forever." Nothing lasts forever: a partner may decide to leave and start their own company, or a partner may decide to quit. Design an easy exit strategy so when the moment comes you, your company, your employees and your clients will not suffer.

- Once the stakes and responsibilities are agreed upon, find a lawyer and have a contract made.

These are sensitive topics, and you might worry that you won't handle them well. If so, get a third party involved, a person with whom everybody is comfortable and who has an unbiased opinion of you and all of your partners. These steps are essential. Once they are done, you will have covered all the vital aspects and potential pitfalls in partnering so you and your team can focus on the business.

Chapter 6

Struggling with Resources and Multitasking

There are too many tasks to list that you will have to manage to make your business a success. In this chapter, we will discuss the most important of them.

Too Much to Do

When you have too many tasks that you need to do in a day, you cannot start tackling them by assigning 5% for a particular task, 10% for another task and so on. You have to address them intelligently and figure out yourself which task you can start now and set that in motion so that you can jump onto another task. Consider the kitchen in a restaurant: the chef does not start cutting vegetables and start preparing meat after the order has been given. Those tasks are already done and he is prepared for orders to come through. So you need to prepare beforehand exactly how you are going to tackle those tasks.

If you are yet to start or if you are a start-up or even a two-year-old small business, you have to take time off from business and plan your tasks in. If you get too busy being busy, you will stop being productive. It is better to position yourself by taking time to prepare for your tasks.

You should anticipate what kind of processes and tasks you will have to do:

- Sales
- Marketing
- Delivery
- Post-delivery
- Hiring
- Support

You need to identify the processes that need to be in place for accomplishing each of these tasks. E.g., have templates of documents and procedures ready to tackle a support issue and have a list of skills and attitudes you require in a person that you intend to hire first. Preparing yourself will help you deal with anticipated tasks, leaving you with time to deal with the unanticipated tasks that crop up. Some tasks do not need your complete attention and shouldn't get it.

Going back to the restaurant kitchen analogy, the chef prepares dishes on several different cookers. He starts to heat up a pan, and while the pan is being heated, he moves on to the next task, getting the ingredients ready. While one dish is being cooked, the chef immediately starts preparing the dish on which the food will be served, and all the while he is looking at the orders to see what he needs to be doing next. And he can do all of this, juggling many dishes at a time, because he is prepared: all his ingredients, recipes, tools, support and procedures are in place.

Compare the chef to a father who doesn't cook and decides to make his children breakfast: he begins by asking, "Where does your mum keep the eggs?" and it all goes downhill from there.

You can be the chef, or you can be the dad, and that difference is all that matters in having smooth running operations within your business; with plenty of time to spare for focusing on business growth related tasks.

Taking a few insights from the above example, you can start applying the same strategy in your life and company. Different cookers mean different people you can delegate your tasks to.

Know Your Company

Do you know your company? Do you know how it operates? Do you know all its organs? As CEO, founder or co-founder of a company, are you fully aware of what operations and processes are involved in your company?

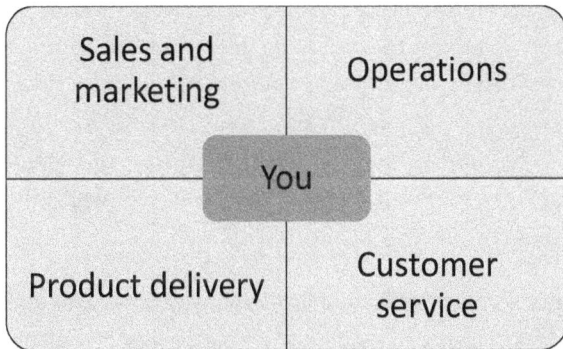

Sales and marketing	Operations
You	
Product delivery	Customer service

4 quadrants of your business

The Unique SMART Analysis™

You need to identify and list all the processes:

- People involved in each of them
- Time required for each operation
- Cost involved

With this list, you will be able to make informed decisions, whether based on marketing or on what is required for entering a new market or if a decision is required to consider delegation or outsourcing. As a CEO, you need to know what are the fundamental list of actions that your company takes is to resolve a problem for the end users.

Delegate

You have to delegate your non-productive work to other people so you can focus on what is important. You need to organise your tasks and priorities. You need to know up front what your return on investment (ROI) of your time and money in regards to the tasks you can carry out is. You need to know why you're about to embark on any given task, and you need to know what you are going to gain by doing it. You need to know how it is going to enrich your current situation and help you. You need to find out if it is necessary for you to do all of them: are there some tasks that you can delegate to other people?

So please, identify how many tasks you are currently doing in your own company and start delegating some of them to other people. Enrich your life with more time and focus on what is necessary at the moment. When you focus on the most important tasks, you will be able to see clearly and use your time and priorities effectively. There are plenty of people to help you; you do not have to have a great amount of money to

58

start delegating work. You can get work for free or at the price you can afford it; all you need is a better strategy.

You do not need funding; you need a better strategy. – Peter Sage

In the early days of being an entrepreneur or in the start-up of your business, you're likely to play different roles. You will have to juggle priorities and resources and tasks in very little time. The trick of getting it right is asking yourself, *"Are you super busy or are you super productive?"* If you have too many tasks, prioritise them into different indexes of benefits. What task is going to give you immediate benefit? What tasks are going to give you immediate success? And what tasks do you love doing? Do the tasks you are passionate about. Try to delegate the rest to others within your team or to your friends or outsource them to somebody.

Quit trying to do things and activities you are no good at and start delegating them. You're wasting your precious time by trying to do activities you are not good at and don't connect to passionately, so start delegating those activities and start focusing on the important tasks you love doing.

Another tip to save time and increase the efficiency of your start-up or small business is to identify any tasks, activities or processes that you do more than once. These processes or activities should have a defined input and an expected output. The steps inside the process tasks can be finite. Identify these processes and tasks. Once you've identified them, create a template of the task's process. Once you have this template, you can delegate the task to anyone in your company.

The fact that it is in a template will assure that the consistency and quality will be higher in comparison to someone not

59

having a template. This will improve your consistency across your company, and efficiency will be improved by achieving the task in little time. The fact that most tasks can be picked up by anyone with a certain prerequisite skill and experience means you will be able to share your responsibilities and spread the workload among your team and employees.

Having a template has two advantages:

1. If you do in the future consider growing in numbers, for example expanding in number of team members, then training them will be easier when assisted by a template.
2. If in the future you consider outsourcing, then this template will help the offshore team in completing your tasks with more accuracy and efficiency.

In the early days of your start-up, you will be overwhelmed with different tasks and responsibilities. You will find yourself multitasking in several domains of your business and working up to sixty hours a week. There is no way to avoid this, but you can make it easier by delegating. You do not have to be one-man army, and to succeed, you can't think of yourself as one.

Simple tasks that you can outsource or delegate:

-   Office-related
    -   Office administration
    -   Call handling
-   Marketing
    -   Stationery design
    -   Brochure design
    -   Email marketing and list management
    -   Online sales letter templates

- Website design
  - o   Web design and development
  - o   Graphic design
  - o   Logo design
- Pre and post-sales management
  - o   Scheduling sales calls
  - o   Scheduling post-delivery follow-up calls
- Social presence
  - o   Social Media
  - o   WordPress / blog management
  - o   Database management
  - o   Content management
- Finances
  - o   Scanning of receipts
- Social gathering
  - o   Ordering of food and cakes
  - o   Organising an office party

The above list is only a few of many tasks that you might come across in your early days of start-up. Try to delegate as much as you can to your team and employees. Look at each member of your new organisation as an engineer sees things.

Why Do You Outsource?

When you decide you want to outsource, you need to first be clear on why you're doing this. 90% of outsourcing projects and delegated tasks fail to meet their intended purpose simply because you have not been clear on the purpose. Some of the common purposes of outsourcing a certain operational task in your company or delegating a certain task to your employees or friends are:

Reasons to outsource
• Saving time
• Saving cost
• Managing resources
• Adding value

So you need to be clear which of these purposes you are aiming at in order to achieve success by outsourcing your process or task.

9 Steps to Successfully Outsource

Reasons to Outsource

1. Identify the reason why you want to outsource.
   a. Is it to reduce costs?
   b. Is it to free your employees to do other important tasks?
   c. Is it to save time?

Plan Your Outsourcing

2. Define the tasks and processes that you are outsourcing. In this step, you need to create a template document which should contain:
   a. Aim of the task
   b. Objective of the task
   c. Prerequisite skills and tools
   d. Inputs
   e. Outputs
   f. Minimum acceptance criteria of quality

Identify the Correct Supplier

3. Choose your provider wisely. Use the answer from step one as the guiding aspect when choosing a provider.
   a. Check their credentials and feedback from other clients.
   b. Check if they can be contacted reliably.
   c. Frequent visits to off-site team (supplier office) means more expense, so you will need to check if it possible to collaborate virtually.
   d. Find out if they believe in your vision and cause.
   e. Find out if they believe in your products and services.
   f. Find out if the language of communication is going to be same.
   g. If they are based in a different country:
      i. Find out about local employment laws.
      ii. Find out about language barriers.

4. Always choose more than one supplier in the early stages of negotiations. This will give you an idea of how each supplier is responding to your questions from step 3.

Mitigate your risks

5. Assess compatibility by narrowing down to two suppliers.
   a. Test their quality.
   b. Test if their end delivery product meets the minimum acceptance criteria.
   c. Check with your team to see if they are happy with the end result.

    d. Listen to your team's key insights as they can easily highlight any discrepancy in the delivery.

    e. It is good to listen to key managers, but more effective is to listen to your front-end team members.

Implementation and Sealing the Deal

6. Sort out legal and payments.

    a. Clarify legal and payment criteria. Link quality to payment terms and conditions.

7. Establish a key bridge person in your company dedicated to liaise with a dedicated member from the offshore team.

    a. Lay out a strict communication protocol to catch up on progress and situations that arise. This should be regularly carried out.

    b. Train another person within your company as a back-bridge person to interact with offshore team.

8. Organise an offshore visit for your team to meet the other team.

9. Document everything you did from step 1

Do not worry when looking at all the steps listed above; there are for your reference and you may not need them. Please choose the appropriate ones that relate to the task you are planning to outsource.

For example, when outsourcing a logo design task, your steps will be simpler as compared to outsourcing a website development project.

Remember, outsourcing does not necessarily mean finding resources in India and China, you do it locally too.

64

My Staff Do Not Understand the Tasks I Give Them to Do

Delegating to people will become your favourite part of doing your tasks. You can achieve this by adding value to the people you work with. You need to groom your team and staff as an extension of you, and to achieve this you need to treat them as you would treat yourself. Add value to their lives and make conscious steps to build a people company.

Focus on What You Have to Do, Not What You Want to Do

Most entrepreneurs spend too much time on the squeaky wheels and putting out fires. It is more important to focus on the main tasks which will get you immediate returns. You need to know how each task is going to benefit you immediately. Know your ROI on tasks upfront; this will save you a lot in resources and time. You have to be much disciplined about choosing your tasks.

Tasks You Have Not Planned For or Not Anticipated

Emergency situations arise in business. This is often the problem when you are initially starting up because you have to strike a balance between how you expand your team and how you grow your brand. If you expand and grow too quickly, you're at the risk the chances of increasing your costs, thus reducing your profits. At the same time, if you expand and grow slowly, you're losing out on new businesses and new clients.

The conventional option to handle sudden rise in work load is to hire contractors. With contractors, you are paying them too much money and in the long run this is not sustainable. I

65

believe outsourcing is the answer for this problem. Your operations can be outsourced both internationally and locally.

View from Top is Great

Stay out of your operations when possible. That way you'll move away from your business and hand tasks over to a good team that can do them better. A successful business owner works *on* his company, not *in* his company. It means you are focused on what's important: growing the business, marketing, making sales and ensuring quality. If you are always inside your business, then your vision will be very short, you're thinking will be very narrow; that can affect your ability to take important strategic decisions. You will very soon burn out.

For example, visualise a football (soccer) game. During the match, the players are on the field playing the game against an opponent. The coach is positioned outside the field of play, and he is much better placed to see all his players, and he is in a much better position to see his opponents and figure out their strategy. During the game, he provides his players with valuable direction and strategy planning. Had the coach been on the field playing along with the players, he would not have been able to provide such valuable insights.

As an entrepreneur or owner of a start-up or a small business, you must get out in the field, play and enjoy the business and guide it to success. But you must also allow yourself the time to take the coach's position: off the field and able to see the big picture.

The other reason for this is you can monitor your company better if you're not on the field with the players. You can see what's happening off the field, just like a good football coach.

66

Socrates once said, *an unexamined life is not worth living.*
In business, you have to examine the processes and the operations of the company. If you're inside the operations too much, you will never be able to examine (and improve) them.

Brand First

You must make sure your brand is present on all documents used in your company: Word documents, Excel spread sheets, email signatures, everything. Your brand must be prominent in all activities and processes that are part of your organisation. To achieve consistency across all documents, save a template document that has your brand in the header, or a cover page or signature file. By saving the message of the brand as a template, you will always achieve consistency and won't have to spend extra effort.

Tools to Get (and Stay) Organised

Some useful tools that can help you to organise your thoughts and ideas:

Evernote

Evernote makes it easy to remember things big and small from your everyday life using your computer, phone, tablet and the web. I use this tool to make note of important tasks for the day, the week ahead and remember monthly goals so I can stay on top of them. The beauty of this application is that you can access your information from any device connected to the internet. You can also record your voice and take photos. This is great tool.

67

Google Documents

Google Drive is a great extension of Google to manage your documents and files. If you do not want to use any of the licenced document editing products, then I would recommend this application from Google. It is a great boon for small businesses. All your documents are stored on the cloud, giving you the benefit of accessing them from anywhere in the world.

Dropbox

Dropbox is a free service that lets you bring all your photos, docs and videos anywhere. This means that any file you save to your Dropbox will automatically save to all your computers, phones and even the Dropbox website. Dropbox also makes it easy to share with others, whether you're a student or professional, parent or grandparent. Even if you accidentally spill a latte on your laptop, have no fear! You can relax knowing that Dropbox always has you covered and none of your stuff will ever be lost.

YouMail

This voicemail service transcribes your voicemail messages and sends them to you by email or text (or both). The mobile app makes it easy to view, listen, read and forward your voice mails.

Sanebox

Automatically filter your email for spam and unimportant messages to only see the emails that are important.

TripIt

TripIt files all your itineraries in one place. You can even have the tool automatically send your itineraries to your business partners. The Pro version alerts you of flight delays and gate changes. Some of the great features are its ability to filter your emails so that you read only that is important to you and you can store your attachments on their cloud network, empowering you to access them from anywhere. There is plenty more which this application can offer you.

Exercise

Keeping your body fit helps you be more active and focused in your business. It will improve your self-confidence and increase your ability to calm your mind. You do not need to build muscles in the gym to get all the benefits of exercise. You have to make sure on a daily basis you raise your pulse rate to its maximum rate possible either by running or cycling for three minutes. Repeat this for three times. Yes, nine minutes is all it takes to feel fresh and focused. *A sound body is a sound mind.*

Meditate

Meditation is one of the best methods to take control of your life and your business. One of the main benefits of meditation is that you learn to focus on the task you are working on by ignoring distractions. In the early days of start-up, it is very easy to get overwhelmed with too much information and the many tasks that need to be done. Meditation will help you keep a calm mind and clear your mind so that you will be able to prioritise on the most important task.

Power does not come by controlling others; true mastery is in controlling your mind.

69

Take a Power Nap

Mind and body do enjoy power naps. Ten minutes of power napping when you are tired will give you an incredible increase of energy and focus. I believe when you are passionate, energetic and calm; people enjoying working with you, clients will see the true passion within you and be convinced to buy your products. Similarly, when your team and employees see you working at a higher level of energy and passion, they get inspired and start to put in more work at the same level as your energy.

I take a ten-minute power nap in the back seat of my car during my lunch break and that powers my afternoon with great energy.

Managing time is easy: you only need to focus on one task at a time and you will see how quickly you can transform your start-up or small business into a great success.

Strength of your team:

No. of operational tasks:

No. of repetitive tasks:

Budget for delegation:

Tasks you are doing at the moment

Tasks you do not like to do in the future

Tasks you would love to do if you had more time

Sites that will help you gain more time

Fiverr.com	Elance.com
Outsourcerr.com	TaskArmy.com
Gigbucks.com	99Designs.com

Which of the above sites did you search for help?

71

Chapter 7

Money Worries

Be tight with money. It has been said that "a dollar saved is three dollars earned," so manage your money effectively. Do not spend it on activities and events which do not add immediate value towards your company. Know your return on investment up front before you spend. Save extra money and use it for a new venture opportunity.

Barter Technique

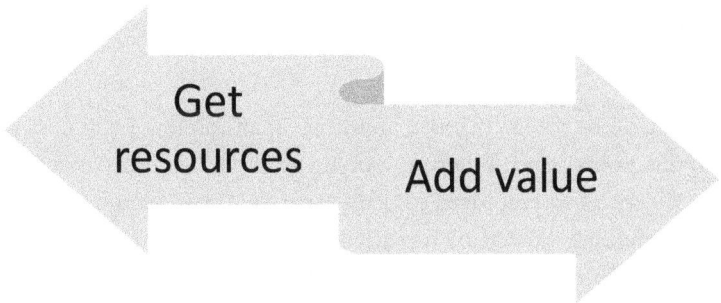

Barter system

Respect and manage money to the last penny, cent or paisa. When you respect money, value it and spend it wisely, you will get more of it. If you have too much money and you don't have to worry about spending carefully, you may soon find yourself in a position that makes you wish you had learned to manage the budget better.

The Unique SMART Analysis™

Too many entrepreneurs overcapitalise their businesses. They believe that one needs a sufficient amount of capital to run a business. That is not always true. Rome was not built in a day. So your business success will not achieve its fullest glory by simply funding it with an enormous amount of money. Business needs time to grow, needs time to establish its brand and needs time to build the right foundation. Without having the right foundation - the right brand, the right vision and the right cause - your business will not be sustainable. You may achieve success overnight, but success built on capital instead of your brand will not last. Perseverance and the right attitude to focus on your strengths are required for your business to succeed.

Everyone is approachable when you have a value to offer. You can approach anyone on this planet when you have something to offer.

A better strategy is more important than money. I will convey this point better by giving you an example from my own life. When I was employed as a test analyst, I was keen to go to a conference hosted by a particular test agency in London. The test conference highlight was talking about agile testing and showcased the latest applications and tools. When I approached the conference organisers to ask how much it would cost, they came back to me with a number I could not afford. My employer didn't believe in training their staff, so there was no budget for training. I was on my own. I asked the organisers and they agreed to a small discount, but it wasn't enough.

So I needed a new strategy, and I got one. I approached the organisers again and told them, "I write articles for my own blog about testing and I take fantastic photos. If you let me in for free I would write at least five articles about your conference and take some photos at your event." This was shot in the dark; I did not expect the organisers to come back with a positive answer. To my surprise, they did. The organisers asked me for examples of my articles and to show them some of my photos.

I forwarded the link to my blog and I showed them some photos I had taken. By the end of the day, they offered me a free ticket to the conference. I was shocked; I never expected it to work. I then remembered Peter Sage's quote – *You don't need money; you need a better strategy.*

So what is it that you need in your company right now for which you have been holding back because you thought you didn't have money to afford it? You need to go back to that list and see if you can try a different strategy and obtain it for free. The barter system still works in today's world. At the end of the day, you're selling products to add value to the other person. And that value does not have to be served by money or time. You can also serve that value with another value. So find out what it is that you can offer to another supplier who would then benefit from your value and also give you something which will then benefit you.

I'll say it again: "You do not need money; you need a better strategy."

Know Your ROI (Return on Investment)

Know your return on investment first. Before you spend time or money on any activity or item, know what value it is going to return. When you have this approach, you will start to filter

75

out activities and start identifying activities that you were previously doing and not gaining any interest or return from.

Second Stream of Income

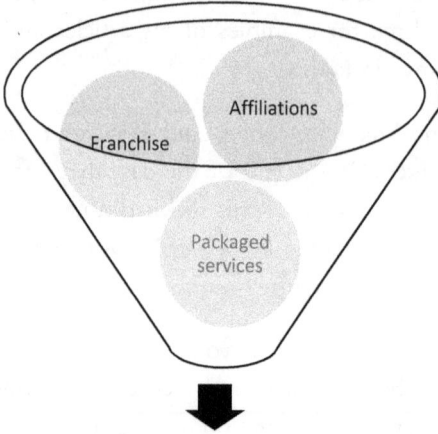

2nd Stream of Income

Second source of incomes

Franchise

Franchising is a great business model to gain momentum and build bridges with other companies in the same industry. Make sure you franchise with the right company in the same industry. When you find the right complementing company whose products and services, when added together with yours, forms a complete package solution for the client, you will start gaining trust of your customers. Also, this can become a second stream of income for you. The revenue you get from franchising other products and services can be used to grow or invest back in the company to innovate more products of your own.

Franchising doesn't always have to be for a bigger-branded company; it can also be a similar-sized or positioned company as yours. The reason you are doing this is to setup a second stream of income and provide a complete solutions package to your clients.

Affiliate Marketing

This is a proven technique for generating extra income. When you decide to opt for franchising, you need to choose the products and services appropriate to your company's products and services. When you add extra complementary products and services to your catalogue, you stand out as an industry expert. When you address your client's problems from A to Z, they feel you are more reliable and as a company, you have thought a lot about understanding your clients.

You need to make sure that your brand identity is always first and top priority; if you start noticing your customers getting confused with your brand to the franchised company's brand, you will have to immediately address that. Remember, affiliations and franchising models are for a secondary income source to enable you to grow your brand with a bit of stability. Never risk the identity of your company's brand.

Packaging Services into New Products

If you're in the industry of providing services, then the amount of money you earn is proportional to the amount of time you have in order to provide the services to your clients. When you're in the service industry, you're often worried about how

77

to make payments: payments to your suppliers, your employees and team members. You get caught up with cash flow problems. One way to avoid this is to have a secondary income source.

When you package your services into a product which can be sold, then you can increase the potential to earn more money without dedicating much of your time towards it. What I mean by packaging your services is to find out if you can extract valuable information about your niche service and apply it into your product. The product could be a book, a mobile application, or a web application hosted on the cloud where a client can purchase your product and access your services themselves. The advantage of having a product which is conceptualisation of your service is that you create a new revenue stream.

78

List the values that you can offer to other businesses:

_____

_____

_____

In which other markets can your product be repackaged as solutions?

79

Chapter 8

A High-Value Business

3 Ingredients of a Great Company

The difference between ordinary and extraordinary is "extra." Extra can be added in several aspects of your business. You can add extra value in enhancing your customer relationships, you can add extra value in engaging your employees and making them feel special for working in your organisation and extra can be adding value to society by being a responsible start-up and small business owner. The three best areas for you to provide extra in are discussed below.

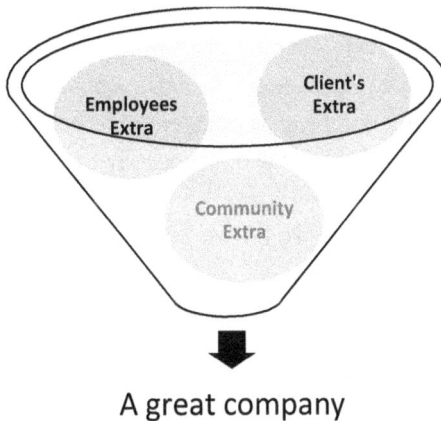

A great company

3 Ingredients of a great company

Extra in End-User Relations

Your end-users buy a certain service or product which you have convinced them adds value to their life or solves a problem that they have. This is ordinary. The extra-ordinary would be to follow up with those clients after the sale has been made to find out if your product or service has achieved its intended purpose. You can do this by phoning them up after couple of days or you can send a letter expressing gratitude and concern to check if they are happy with your service and product. You go further extra and send seasonal greeting cards or birthday cards. By adding this extra effort to your customer relationship process, you are maintaining that connection with that customer and providing an extra value on top of the value you're already providing via your service and products.

Extra in Employee Relations

Your employees do their work for you with great interest and passion and you provide salary in exchange for the work. This is the ordinary and normal process which every employer does. The extra-ordinary employer would engage their employees and team members by providing opportunities to grow, provide training to become better leaders. The extra-ordinary employer offers extra responsibilities other than the employees intended roles, activities they love and that lets them know they are valued.

Extra in Community Relations

As a responsible business owner, you pay taxes and the government provides the required infrastructure and legal procedures to facilitate and protect your business. This is ordinary. When you make an extra effort to support the community you live in, that is extra-ordinary. It can be as simple as supporting a local charity, supporting a local school team or it can even be encouraging your staff to take part in charity events. Support a cause, get involved in your local community charities or support a global charity.

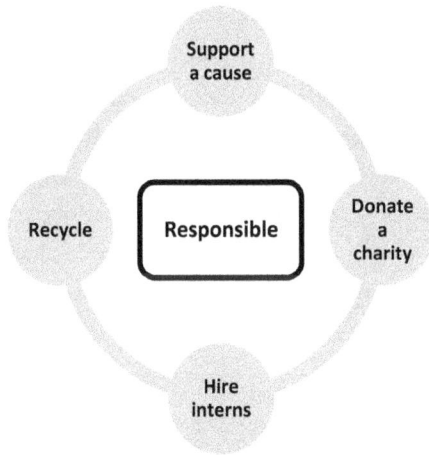

The responsible brand

Motivation and Vision

Motivation is the key ingredient of a true entrepreneur. You need motivation to inspire your teams; you will need motivation to achieve success and stay focused on the target. One of the simplest and effective techniques to maintain focus and stay motivated is to have a vision. When you have a vision, motivation, inspiration and aspiration comes with it. So what is your vision?

The Unique SMART Analysis™ highlights the importance of having a vision statement for the company because a vision statement is more focused towards the end goal. It addresses

83

the values which will benefit the end user and clients; it simultaneously creates a passionate drive for your employees to work extra hard for your company because they believe that their effort contributes towards a great cause beyond the numbers in the annual profit report.

Do not have mission statements. It is a waste of time. A mission statement usually focuses on the shareholders and the market; it rarely addresses the end goal of the company. It is more of an itinerary for the trip rather than talking about the destination or reason for the journey. You will spend too much time and money in deriving one. The only people who are going to benefit from having a mission statement are the contractors you hire in assisting you in forming a mission statement.

Reward Your Team to Grow

The best reward you can offer to your employees is an opportunity for them to improve their skills and learn new ones. Provide them with opportunities to carry out research and development to develop new and innovative products, encourage your employees to attend industry related conferences and allow your employees to fail and learn. Facilitate a working culture where employees can improve themselves and take on new challenges different from their ordinary roles. Remember, you cannot get to your goals alone: you need to have the strength and spirit of all your team members and employees to achieve success. If you want your company to grow and expand and gain greater success, you need to encourage growth within your own company.

84

Reward Your Team with a Great Culture

You need to socially engage with your employees to be part of your company culture. Get them involved with all aspects of your company, especially the vision, cause and brand. A great way to engage your employees and to promote their contributions to the company is by having an internal forum, a forum exclusively for your employees. The forum can have one or two sections that talk about the company's vision or cause. In this forum, your employees can choose any topic they want and start adding their opinions and sharing interesting topics and articles. Some employees might also want to write an article themselves. If enough employees like to write articles, you might consider having an article of the month to be published on your company website. This will engage your employees in the same direction as your company by rewarding them for providing extra commitment to the company. Everybody likes a challenge; provide a challenge to employees and team members and make them more interested in your company.

We hang around a lot of times off-business. We do plenty of activities together. As an entrepreneur I got to choose the people I want and love to work with and hang around. From the company's side we celebrate each and everyone's birthdays and personal events; a voucher or gift or benefits are provided in order to celebrate the occasion. – Dr.Nagachetan

After a stressful project de-stress your team and employees by giving them a day off. Consider taking them for: go-karting, paintballing or laser combat. Taking part in activities like these, your employees get to release their stress and get happier. The advantage of involving your team and employees in such activities is that it also acts as a team-bonding exercise. You

85

don't have to wait for an annual event, such as a Christmas party or a summer party to organise such events. You can organise these events at any at any point in the year. This is a great way of relieving stress and encouraging team-bonding.

If your team is small, between fifteen and twenty members, you might institute a company lunch once a week or once a month. Sharing a meal is a good way for employees to bond and to discuss the company's direction and vision in an informal setting.

"Gamify"[9] your meetings and engage everyone involved in the meeting. Chairing and managing a conventional meeting can be boring. A traditional meeting approach may not encourage everyone on the team to contribute to discussions. By adding an extra game element to the meeting, more people will get involved and contribute.

Engage with Innovation

Have programs within the company to encourage innovation and motivate everyone in the company to come up with new ideas. This is a great way to empower leadership and responsibility in everyone. And have great rewards for those who are contributing to this.

A great new product or a great new service that can be introduced as part of the company portfolio is a boon to the company. The reward for the originator of a new idea might be a percentage from the profit the company would make from the product or service to the winning team member. This kind of incentive will result in many valuable new ideas.

---

[9] Further reading *Gamestorming: A Playbook for Innovators, Rulebreakers, and Changemakers* by Dave Gray, Sunni Brown and James Macanufo

Reward your employees

Did you know that Gmail was a product of Google's initiative to build entrepreneurs within the company? Gmail was developed by Google's 23rd employee, Paul Buchheit, was passionate about building an email service and Google's founders believed in nurturing creativity and entrepreneurship within the company. They provided the resources and funding needed to build an email service and the rest is history. Even though Google started off as a search engine, their founders have consistently inspired and empowered their own staff to come up with new products.

A similar technique is used by LinkedIn, where every employee is given the opportunity to come up with an idea on how to improve the current product and add more value to it so the end-user is benefited. The employees of LinkedIn are given

87

three months to go away and develop functionality, and at the end of the three months the employee is given an opportunity to present the new functionality in front of their manager, the CTO or even the CEO. LinkedIn has a culture of encouraging innovation, by involving everyone in the company. This way they're also planting the seeds of future leaders.

Grow expertise within your own company. Plant seeds and invest in your team members and employees. Identify key people who are willing to grow and become leaders and responsible contributing employees. Once you identify these employees, you can encourage them to participate in team meetings or contribute to key decision-making events. You can encourage them to go and attend industry related conferences. You need to grow expertise within your company and to embed your company culture, your company's vision, your company's values and, most importantly, a part of your own self in these employees. When you do this, you are achieving greater productivity and laying roads for future growth and expansion of the company. You need to start working on this from day one. Start identifying people who can be a potential manager, a potential leader or potential expert.

As we look ahead into the next century, leaders will be those who empower others. – Bill Gates[10]

Our approach is constant and never-ending strategic innovation and improvement in the area of machine vision, pattern recognition, signal processing and its allied applications – Dr. Nagachetan[11]

---

[10] Bill Gates – Co-founder of Microsoft.

[11] Dr.Nagachetan – CEO and co-founder of Visio Ingenii

88

Share Your Rewards

Share the rewards of business with all your team members and employees. When you have achieved a milestone or achieved a great success that was not anticipated, then share it with everyone involved. It doesn't have to be annual bonuses or great benefits in terms of medical insurance, dental insurance or providing a company car or company mobile. I'm talking about rewards which will make them feel special, like giving everybody a team coffee mug, or giving them a chance to print their own saying on a company T-shirt. Make everyone feels special and part of a great family, one that is connected by a single vision and cause.

Build a great culture in the company. Remember, it is your company: if you do not make an effort to make it a better place and care about your employees, who will? If you're wondering what I'm talking about, imagine yourself as a king in a distant land and the company is your land. Your employees are your subjects and citizens. Kings from other neighbouring lands come and pay homage to you when they see how your brand is thriving. People from other lands will talk about how great it is to live in a land governed and protected by you, the noble king.

Attracting the Right People

When you're interviewing people for your team, you need to find out why they want to join your company. You need to look for the killer instinct, to find out if they are they a seeker. No matter what positions they have achieved in the past and no matter what responsibilities they have handled in the past or what type of skills that they have acquired in the past, all of this is immaterial if they do not believe in getting more out of life.

89

The best employees are believers in your brand. The new hire should believe in your brand, your vision and the cause. Another important characteristic to look at when you're hiring people is the adaptability skill. This adaptability skill is a very niche and very important skill to look for. Anyone can be a specialist or a certified professional; the trick is how one can transfer those skills and transfer the professional expertise they have gained and apply them to different tasks or different products. Almost anyone can learn or acquire a new skill. Being adaptable is applying the skills to other aspects of your business.

Domain Expertise Is Highly Overrated

As an entrepreneur, you are looking to make new things by taking pieces from here and there and assembling them in a novel way. In this process, magic happens in the intersection; magic happens when two things combine. If you hire a person who is only a domain expert, their thinking is very narrow. They will struggle to adapt their skills to other parts of the system, or they will struggle to transfer their skills to other technologies. What you need to have is a person with an adaptable attitude to transfer any skills they have into any domain or any technology to make things happen. You may need domain expertise later in your business when you are established, but when you're starting a business, you need the agility to absorb new technologies and new trends. Having only domain expertise will make it difficult to achieve that business agility. If you believe in expertise, then please hire experts later, not at the beginning.

Support and Grow Your Company's Vision

As a company, you will have a vision governed by the market or industry you are targeting. If you do not have a vision, then you are lost.

In today's companies, the most common mistake in their reward system is they only include monetary benefits like bonuses, cars, pensions, health care, dental care and phones. Employees like these rewards, but they are never strong enough to drive them to do a better job.

To build a great company, it is vital to achieve the 3Gs of an entrepreneur.

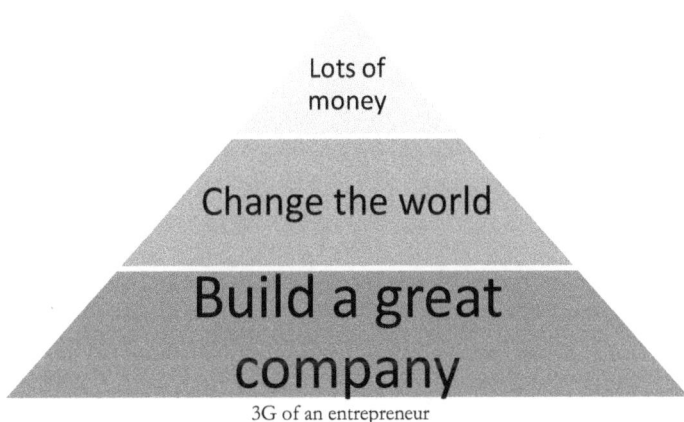

Lots of
money

Change the world

Build a great company

3G of an entrepreneur

Good brands reflect the histories of the time and the group of people that made them. They cannot be copied. They cannot be recycled.
- Sir Richard Branson

Even with the best product; people need to trust you. Trust was built by promising reality, presentation was practical; my passion was embedded in every presentation – Dr.Nagachetan

What does your brand stand for?

_____

_____

_____

What is your company's vision and cause?

_____

_____

_____

List all the social activities organised in your company for the last 6 months:

```
┌─────────────────────────────────────────┐
│                                           │
│                                           │
│                                           │
│                                           │
│                                           │
└─────────────────────────────────────────┘
```

List all the charities your company supports:

```
┌─────────────────────────────────────────┐
│                                           │
│                                           │
│                                           │
│                                           │
│                                           │
└─────────────────────────────────────────┘
```

92

Chapter 9

How to Get Noticed

If you get your face and your name out there enough, people will start to recognize you. - Richard Branson

Your existing services or products must be advertised in a way that highlights the solution they provide to a particular niche market. When you have a market niche, you know what type of clients and customers you're attracting. When you focus on providing a solution, it will enable you to understand your clients better. When you understand your clients better, you'll get to know their problems, their priorities, their lifestyles, their behaviours and their geographical locations. This will help you to target your services and products by addressing these valuable points.

When you target your clients and audiences by addressing their priorities, their lifestyles, behaviours and their problems, you will connect to them on an emotional level. If you connect to them on an emotional level, they will buy your product. They will trust you. This will give you an edge in marketing and when planning to grow your company. This will give you insights about where to expand. It will also clarify what kind of partners, what type of investors and what type of outsourcing companies to approach.

The Importance of Your Brand

Quality brands never go bankrupt. - Richard Branson

In the short time that you have been in business, you will have noticed by now that people do business with people they like. This means your products and your services are appealing to the end-users in solving their problems. And your solutions should be unique and must have an identity that refers back to you and your identity. Your identity in the business world is called a **brand**. This is how you differentiate yourself from other service providers, other industries and your competitors. Your brand enables you to stand out and get noticed. In this early stage, you must build your brand identity, nourish it with consistent and unique marketing, quality and timely deliverance, have a strong vision with objective goals and superior customer service. These aspects of your business are the key ingredients to grow a strong brand, a great brand. But be aware:

With a great brand comes great responsibility

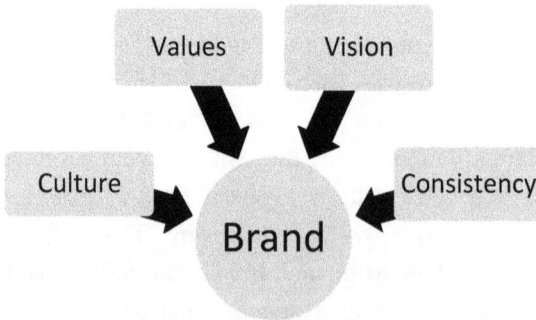

A great brand

94

A service starts with a promise. A great service is not a service until it costs you something. You need to ensure the promises you make are matched by promises you keep.

Your brand should stand out as an icon, the North Star for those who are seeking services and products. This brand will lead your customers to you. You have to build this brand while your company is still young. You need to strictly monitor how your brand is received in the market, recognised by people and seen by people.

Don't be a Jack-of-all-trades and master of none. Identify your key skills and key market and know the strengths of your team members and employees and focus on your strengths and your skills. Avoid trying to get into all kinds of markets; avoid talking about all sorts of problem solving. Become a master of one and brand it.

The SMART™ Service

Identify the key 10% of your returning clients. Find out why they are returning to buy more products. Find out more about them, their location and the benefits they get from using your product. To get this kind of feedback from your 10% of returning clients, you may have to provide a special deal or attract them with a special free service or product. Build a special connection with these people. Send seasonal cards to them, collect their birthdays or anniversaries and send special emails or a letter wishing them well on these special days. Connect with them on an emotional and personal level. Your product is already achieving the emotional connection with them; it is time as a company for you to connect to them on a personal level. This connection will go a very long way. 10% of

95

your clients will share their special experience with you to ten people or more. They will share it on their Facebook page, they will tweet about it, or they will submit a post on Google+. Great customer service is the cheapest marketing a company can get.

Companies can boost profits by 75-100% by retaining as few as 5% of their current customers. - Harvard Business Review

Most companies would rather be certain they're average than risk being greater. – Chinmai Swamy

Customer Testimonials

If you have an existing client base, approach a few of them and ask if they're willing to give your products a testimony in exchange for a free service or a free product. Mention to them that this testimony of theirs will be published on your website and other social media platforms. Also ask for any successful stories from your customers: what type of emotional benefit or monetary benefit or protective benefit they achieved by using your service or using your product.

A survey is commonly used in the market for getting insights about products and services from your clients. You can get effective and simple testimonials from your clients by providing a list of potential problems they face, a list of potential solutions that your product or service can solve, and a list of potential emotional benefits your products and services has provided. This way, your clients only have to go through a simple list and select an item to provide you with a perfect testimony. When you provide them these lists, always give them the option to change and edit any of their testimonials at will.

96

Making Money Is about Adding Value

The Unique SMART Analysis™ understands that people buy your products and services because they believe that buying your product or service is going to make an impact on their lives by solving a problem or satisfying a need. They believe that your product can add value, whether emotional value or financial value, or both. It is this value that convinces them to buy your product or service. Without value, you cannot make money. You can have the best car in the world, but if your brand is not about delivering a certain type of value, then you will always struggle to convince the end-user to consume it. You need to ask what value your products and services are adding to the clients.

Create a Great Social Presence

You should create an audience that will like you and talk about you and share your company's services and products. Previously, the only marketing was off-line marketing. In today's world, you can achieve better results by having a great online social presence. You need to talk about your brand, your solutions and the emotional value which you add to the market on your social media channels. This is how you build a great audience. People will not like your Facebook page, will not follow your Twitter account and will not add you to their circle in Google+ simply because you have a great product or simply because you have a great brand. They will follow *you*; they will like you and add you to their circles depending on what emotional value you are adding with your services and products. You need to have accounts on Twitter, Facebook and Google+. These three are a fundamental requirement by which you can spread your social presence to other social

97

communities. Refer to my *Time to Take Action* chapter to see how you can achieve this with a single click of a button. In this chapter, I will show you how you can organise your posts and share them across different social media channels with a single click.

Have Separate Social Media Presences

You need to make sure you have different social media presences for your company, your brand, your vision, your products and services. Examples of different accounts are:

CEO account: this is a personal. Here you tweet and post about your personal life and you interact with your friends and family. Here you tweet about your state of mind, your beliefs, your passions and share your photos from your recent travels.

Company account: this is a company-to-client tweet about activities within the company and news about the company.

Company offers: in this account, you tweet about special offers to attract clients and you tweet about asking for feedback from existing clients. You tweet about your latest products and services. You can use this account to test the waters when you're about to launch a new product or service and quickly gain feedback from clients and users.

Company free tips and services: in this account, you tweet and post about how your products and services solve a particular problem or fulfil a particular need in the market. In this account, you offer free advice on how a client can resolve problems or find alternatives.

98

An Innovative Way to Create a Need in the Market

It is often the case that when you enter into a market with your products and services you will find it hard to convince customers to buy them. In most cases, the reason why customers don't buy your product is that they do not know what that product can do for them and do not know why that product was introduced in the market.

If you and your company are currently facing a similar situation, you can learn something from what Red Bull did in their early days: they created an artificial need in the market.

This is the story of how Red Bull developed their brand by leaving empty cans in nightclubs. When Red Bull was launched, few knew what Red Bull was and what it had to offer. So the CEO hired a bunch of college students and asked them to carry empty cans in their coat pockets when they went to nightclubs. The students were instructed to leave behind the empty cans in the corners of the nightclubs. Nightclub owners concluded Red Bull must be very popular and knew they were not selling it. They then approached the company and asked them to start supplying them with Red Bull. This is the way Red Bull created a need in the market. So be innovative when it comes to introducing your value and solution into the market.

This is similar to what Apple achieved unintentionally by introducing white colour ear-buds for their iPods; by introducing a different colour, they artificially created a curiosity in the market amongst non-customers.

99

Engage with Your Customers

As a CEO of the company, you need to directly engage with your customers and find out how they're being enriched by the values and the services you are providing. You can do this by writing a letter to a customer who had recently expressed their dissatisfaction in your services and products. Let them know you are concerned with their experience and that you are serious about improving it. You, as the CEO and the leader of the organisation, need to make time and directly build relationships with your customers.

You can also send a letter of thanks to your recent customers. When you are small and your client numbers are growing, this activity might seem not scalable. But it is important as a small business and a start-up for you to incorporate these activities from day one. Remember: great customer service is the cheapest marketing you can get. So think what activity you can do today which will directly engage with the end-user. Remember, engaging is not talking about your product or service; engaging is connecting to them by addressing their needs and adding value in their lives.

Give Back to Your Community

SMART™ promotes and strongly advocates companies to support a charity. You, your employees and your clients are first and foremost human beings, and humanity is the underlying connection between all three of you. By supporting a charity, you not only get great business advantages, you also make the world a better place.

Donate to a charity every month and proudly advertise the fact that you are supporting a charity on your website. When you

100

say that you are supporting a charity or cause, the image of your company is improved. It creates an impression that you are responsible company and you believe in making the society around you better. Remember, people do business with people they like. This may be the extra factor which will convince a potential customer to buy your service or product. Position yourself as a responsible start-up or small business.

Business Is Built on Relationships, Not Products

People who serve the most get the most. You have to serve first to attract purchases. If you start pitching your products and services first and don't talk about the end-user's problems and concerns, if the focus is all about you, then you will not achieve the success you want.

Establish a relationship with potential customers first before you discuss your products. Find out why the person is having the problem or need. Find out more about that person. Then help them pick the product from your company so he can buy directly. This will establish you as an industry expert and as an excellent customer service provider. We have already learned that being an industry expert earns you more attention and makes you stand out from the sea of sameness, and excellent customer service provides you free marketing. You need to capitalise on every opportunity when a client knocks on your door asking for help.

If the concern voiced by the end-user is not directly related to your product or services, do not turn them away. Build a relationship with the person first; find out more information as to why the person needs that service or product. Go out of your way and come up with solutions so that you can go back to the customer with the solutions. When you do this, you

101

again stand out as an industry expert and as an excellent customer service provider. In this case, you're standing out as an industry expert by being a responsible service provider. You are displaying an act of service to the end-user, and with great customer service comes great free marketing.

Values Marketing Makes You Visible

Invisibility is the most common challenge faced by start-ups and small businesses. You are invisible when people only know you by your product and not by your values. If you drive your company's marketing strategy by advertising products, you will always remain invisible. On the other hand, if your marketing strategies are driven by values (the way you enrich the market and the problems you address) then you will be visible. People need to know what you do for them.

Focus Your Efforts

You cannot be a one-stop shop for everything. The end-user will see you as a company that doesn't have any idea what it is. You need to find your micro-niche and stand out as an industry expert in that niche alone. When you focus on one particular niche, you can charge any premium for the services and products you sell. The fact that you are focused on one particular niche uses the advantage of portraying yourself as an expert in that field. Remember: you always pay more for a specialist doctor in comparison to a general practitioner who treats all ailments. And a doctor that specialises in a specific area of your body earns more because the doctor has focused on one particular micro-niche. As we have discussed previously, Apple's successes in the last ten years are due to its consistent focus on its micro-niche: superior and end-user-centred design.

102

As a company, you have to decide if you would like to earn more or if you would like to earn an average amount of money. Package your services and products and sell them to a particular niche market attracting a very particular type of client by amplifying a very particular type of emotional value and benefit your products and services will provide and you will earn great money from it.

You choose the way you dress depending on what features of your body you want to highlight also based on what type of event you're attending. This is an analogy that I like to use when it comes to marketing your services and products. When you have an opportunity to present your services and products to a particular group, you have to carefully pick and choose the services and products which you believe will enrich the particular group. You have to make sure you don't talk about all the solutions and all the values you add. Doing that is like wearing a tuxedo over your favourite sweater over your favourite football jersey. It's too much. You have to choose a few, or, if possible, only one solution to present to that particular group of clients.

Build an Ecosystem for Your Customers

A great way to engage your customers and clients and to get great feedback is by hosting a Google hangout. In these hangouts, you can approach your end-users to talk about the new solutions and new values which you have contributed to the market. You can also talk about your existing solutions and values you are bringing into the market. You need to make sure these hangouts occur at the same time and the format of these hangouts is consistent. You need to have a defined objective of what you want to achieve and also you need to convey straightaway to the end-user what they are going to gain by contributing and attending your hangout. Google+ has provided this great platform to revolutionise the way start-ups and small businesses interact with their clients and end-users.

An ecosystem of your own

Another great way to get feedback is by having a YouTube channel. In this channel, you will showcase your services and your products, talk about the value you bring, the vision statements of your company, the solutions you provide and what the benefits of purchasing your solutions are. You can have all of these mentioned in different small video clips. You need to make sure your videos are between two to three minutes long, because the moment you hit more than three minutes, you're losing out on people who do not have the patience to watch to the end. If you shorten your video to less than two minutes, then people may think there isn't enough content, so they just scroll on.

The advantage of having a YouTube channel showcasing your

104

services and products and also showcasing your latest innovation is for people to look at them and comment. You will get live free feedback from end-users and potential clients simply because you have advertised them on YouTube. And you know the potential of having a YouTube success; you might have the next video to have 1 billion hits.

Focus on your niche and deliver it with precision. How did Apple achieve global dominance in tablet devices and touchscreen phones? They focused on their niche – the perfect user experience – and with that they sold a dream to their end-users. They were not the first in the tablet industry, neither were they first in the touchscreen industry, but when they did arrive they focused on values and services. They did not target everybody in the world, but only the ones who wanted a different experience in comparison with existing products. This is SMART™ as discussed in this book: providing quality services to end users.

How is your brand recognised?

_____

_____

_____

List of social media accounts: e.g. Facebook, Twitter

_____

_____

_____

Your best customer testimonials:

How do you interact with customers after the sale?

The Unique SMART Analysis™

Chapter 10

I Am Trying to Grow the Business, but It's Not Working

"Without continual growth and progress, such words as improvement, achievement, and success have no meaning." - Benjamin Franklin

Three Ways to Grow and Establish Your Brand

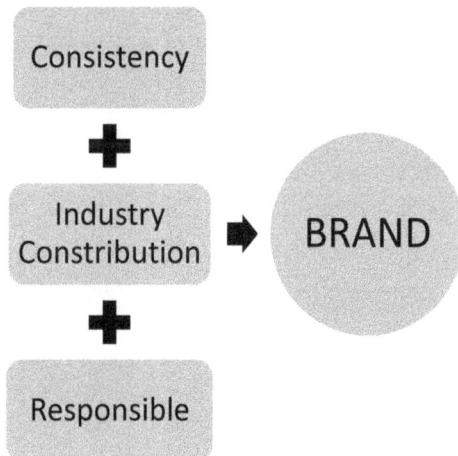

3 variables for a successful brand

107

Achieving Consistency

How people refer to your business is crucial. If five out of five people talk about your business in the same way or they are able to explain what you as a business do in the same way, you are branded.

Contributing to Your Industry

Establish yourself within the industry by going to conferences and presenting research papers; your brand recognition will grow. You can also present a **case study** and highlight what you as a business have achieved and contributed to your end user.

Being Responsible

Support a charity and a global cause like eradicating poverty, solving clean water scarcity water in Africa or Oxfam. Volunteer in your local council and government agency programs which are involved in training young graduates and students to become young entrepreneurs, like "Working Knowledge" in the UK.

Adapting to Newer Markets

When you have a service and product which has worked in the past, you need to next strategically adapt that success to other markets. You may not have to create another idea or another product.

What you can do to start is to ask yourself these questions:

- What can your service do beyond what it was designed to do?
- What can your product do beyond what it was designed to do?
- What kind of clients and customers has this product worked for? Who else can it help?
- If it has worked in one country, can it also work in another country? Or, why is it not working in another country?

If your small business is already established, it has a brand which is well-known. The brand is consistent and your clients and customers know what the brand is about. The company is established as a market expert for solving a particular niche problem in the market. That is good. To take this success further, you need to evolve your brand into other products and markets.

Agility Facilitates Brand Evolution

When you plan to launch a new enterprise or launch a new product to target a different market niche, then you need to have a different brand. You grow by evolving your brand from one successful brand to the next.

Let's consider a hundred-year-old brand, Coca-Cola. Part of Coke's brand is a red can. When Coke wanted to offer products with less sugar, it did not change the constitution of the existing Coke by reducing sugar. Coke launched a new product called Diet Coke and it had a different colour scheme. Coke's original brand did not change. Coke wanted to serve, attract and bridge an existing gap in the market, so it launched

109

a separate product. It even had a different colour to attract a different type of clients.

Similarly, when Coke wanted to attract clients in India, it found out that Indians prefer more sugar and so it launched a different drink called Thumbs Up. The 100-year-old legacy of red colour Coke is still untouched, and Coke continues to introduce new products. That is brand evolution at its best.

Build a Community

Build a community for your clients to interact in. This will help them exchange information about their problems and how your solutions have solved them. This will help them communicate with other people around the world who are facing the same problems. By doing this, you will build a community by which you can attract other clients other potential customers to join.

To build upon a community, you can then offer a sale to encourage new community members to join. A community has a huge potential for you to improve your products, release new products and get quick feedback. Tap into the new power source of crowdsourcing. This will give you huge benefits like marketing and feedback. This gives you a chance to improve your customer relationships, get new ideas, find potential affiliates and partners and also maybe potential new employees or team members.

Think Globally

Find out how you can grow your business globally either by franchising or finding partners from other parts of the world. You will have to find the right like-minded people to achieve

110

going global. The only way to attract like-minded people and partners is to have a vision that will call other people from other industries to work with you.

- Franchising is a great way to go global.

- Partnering with another company in another part of the world is another way to go global.

- Making your products available online, packaged and ready to be shipped is another way of going global

- Having a .com domain is a must if you're going to have a global presence for your company.

Mentors and Coaches

Everybody needs a coach or mentor, even you. The greatest sports star would be just another athlete without a great coach. A coach seizes the potential inside you and trains your strengths. A coach focuses on your positives and strengths to bring out the best within you. A coach will guide you to success by simply observing your strengths and stirring your activities towards the goal you want to achieve. In this process, a coach remodels your habits, reprograms your attitude and focuses on your strengths and sets new behaviours within you. Even if you're at an early stage of becoming an entrepreneur or starting a start-up or already heading a small business, you need a coach to achieve a greater goal and enjoy the path of success.

Find a coach within your industry. It can be a friend or a professional coach or a business coach who can advise you on what tasks you should focus on. The coach will highlight the priorities you should immediately address and the coach will lay a path of success for you to walk. And most importantly, a

111

coach will work with you and monitor your progress and highlight if you are straying from your goal.

Having a coach is only half the work because you need to play your part too. You need to actively participate in your success program. You need to change your state of mind and believe in the coach, and you need to believe that the coach will lead you to success. Any amount of time spent with your coach, however brief it may be, will be beneficial.

A coach strengthens you; a mentor guides you. To grow your business, you need both.

Mind the GAP

You also need to have a GAP document. GAP stands for goals, assumptions and processes.

Goals

What goals you can achieve in the next year or six months.

Assumptions

Assumptions are what you think you know about your goals.

Processes

Processes are what steps, actions and tasks you need to take to achieve your goals.

From time to time, you will have to do an exercise called "mind the GAP." This exercise identifies your processes and departments, services and products which are preventing you from reaching your goals. You need to make sure you involve all your employees in this exercise. If your company has too

112

many employees then you need to devise a way where all employees can contribute to this exercise, either by sending an email to you or to a specific email address. The reason I suggest involving everyone in your start-up and small business to be part of this "mind the gap" exercise is that it's beneficial to have different opinions from different contexts. Different employees view the challenges from a different perspective and you cannot afford to miss out on any of them.

GAP – Goals, Assumptions and Processes

Repeat Success

Take one successful client you have provided great value to and see how you can relive the magic and apply the same emotional bonding with different clients and to attract more clients.

If you have achieved success in servicing and adding value in your one particular market and you can reapply the same magic into another domain or enter into another market. This is great because now you will diversify and become an expert in a new industry. This is doable, but you have to do it right.

113

- Don't launch a new product under the same old website.
  Don't try to attract different-market clients under the same
  website.

You cannot talk about a new solution or a new product or try
to attract different types of clients through the same existing
brand. You need to have a different website and you need to
have a different logo to promote the new brand.

You can associate your parent brand with the new brand, but
no content from the parent brand should be made available on
the new site. You must also have a new domain. Because you
are targeting a different set of clients, you need to have a
different showroom.

The great success cycle

Do identify which micro-market you would like to address.

Do buy a domain which symbolises that market and your new
product and newly-packaged product.

114

Do create a new website with different colour schemes to attract new clients. To start off with, you can have the designs and themes from your existing website. This can save a bit of money, but just try and change the colours so that it will look different.

Do have a different email address for the end-user to contact.

Go Back to Your Business Plan

You need to take time at least twice a year and revisit your business plan. You need to do this because you can check your progress and measure your progress. You need to do this to see if you're on course. You need to see if you have the same vision and passion you had when you wrote the document. You need to evaluate if any of those goals are not practical in regard to the current market.

A business plan is like a map. The smaller the map, the more precise the map is. Your business plan must be short and concise, easy to read and understand, with no technology or complex business words used. Your business plan should be easy to read; it must be consistent with respect to fonts and font sizes.

Your business plan is a self-monitoring tool for sales and recruitment. When you revisit your business plan, you also need to make a few important checklists:

✓ Do you need a new financial plan, or are you okay with what you started with on day one?
✓ Check to see if you can create a new product or service.

115

- ✓ Check if your plan reflects the reality that is your current circumstances.
- ✓ Are there any changes in the market?
- ✓ Have any of your partners or investors left the company?
- ✓ Any change in the way your business is now running? Ad-hoc processes and work-around solutions can become mainstream operations.

You need to ensure everything is functional as per plan.

Trying to Expand or Grow Too Quickly?

Grow! But one brand at a time. Before you start developing new products or entering into new markets, you need to first establish yourself in one market and in one product. You need to establish a one-brand market and industry. If you try to make your presence felt all over the place, then you will very soon see your company going downhill. The disadvantage of having too many markets or diversifying too quickly is that you're sending out mixed signals to your end-user. When you confuse your potential clients and end-users, you will not attract them and convince them to buy your product or services. So establish yourself first as one single brand, one in which you're consistent in delivering quality services.

Work with Other Brands

To grow your brand, you need to start working with other brands by collaborating with them or partnering with them. When you work with another brand, you add value to your brand and add value to their brand as well. When your brand grows, talented people will want to work with you, investors will want to work with you and, most importantly, you will attract clients.

116

I Am Trying to Grow the Business, but It's Not Working

Be Out to Grow

If you are interested in growing your company and going public or seeking investment, then as a CEO and founder you need to build a company which can operate without you involved in any more than three operations. You have to grow your company with an attitude of being out of it. Your involvement in the company should only be at the top strategic decision making level and not operational. Investors do not like this because you are too involved in the company and too much risk is tied to your involvement in the company.

New Processes

As a start-up you may want to start with one process, but in your downtime try out new processes because you can never say what type of client will next knock on your door. Taking the concept of having different processes forward, you will have to think about a similar situation in your industry and think of different possible clients you might encounter, and when you do encounter them, what services can your start-up provide so you will stand out as an industry expert.

For example, if you are a software development start-up that is developing applications for smart devices, then your processes must range from:

- **Waterfall model** - Long projects where the client is happy to see you once a month and needs to see the end result.

- **Kanban** – Short projects that need to be done quickly, within three to four months. The requirements for this project are not fully submitted at once; the client is busy and cannot provide the entire spectrum of

117

The Unique SMART Analysis™

requirements at once and will provide it in smaller chunks.

- **Scrum** – The client is very hands-on and likes to interact more often than other clients. He likes to see progress at regular intervals. He wants the project delivered in less than a month or two.

As an IT company, you will have to deal with all three types of clients. You need to provide different processes to your team as guidance to progress on each of the projects. You can achieve this through the same team if they have the right direction. Train your team in all three types of development so that they can hop in and hop out each of them as the project demands. Most importantly, you need to have an excellent leader to guide your team. One who has the passion to do so, and one who is driven by a desire to handle challenges on a daily basis.

Focus on the Road Ahead

Things change because we live in an ever-changing world. Take small steps based on what has worked in the past and move ahead. A closed mind sacrifices knowledge and opportunities. Wisdom is learning from every situation regardless of outcome.

118

I Am Trying to Grow the Business, but It's Not Working

*Sensei told the monks this morning that the reason we can't walk or run backwards easily or comfortably is because we aren't supposed to be doing anything backwards. Sensei said, '**Just focus on what lies ahead. Thinking backwards or regretting your past is just not natural and that's why it feels uncomfortable.**'* - Unknown

The Unique SMART Analysis™

Make a list of industry-related conferences held in your city. Plan to visit at least one in the next 6 months.

Mind the GAP

Your company GOALS for this year:

```
┌─────────────────────────────────────────┐
│                                         │
│                                         │
│                                         │
│                                         │
│                                         │
└─────────────────────────────────────────┘
```

Your assumptions / analysis of the goals:

```
┌─────────────────────────────────────────┐
│                                         │
│                                         │
│                                         │
└─────────────────────────────────────────┘
```

What PROCESSES are required to achieve them?

```
┌─────────────────────────────────────────┐
│                                         │
│                                         │
│                                         │
│                                         │
└─────────────────────────────────────────┘
```

The Unique SMART Analysis™

Chapter 11

The Website Is Getting Hits, but No One Is Buying ☹

This chapter addresses ways to improve online sales.

Solutions, Not Products

If your website is getting a lot of traffic but not making many sales, you may be too focused on your products. Talk to your clients about their problems and see how you can connect to them emotionally. Talking about your products is not going to get their attention. You need to advertise your solutions in a way that you can communicate to them on an emotional level, a reason for them to buy your product or service. You are not providing a product: you are providing a solution.

Some bad examples of products and services pages read like this:

"We develop mobile applications on all platforms."

"We have a global presence."

"Our products are industry-standard certified."

121

"We have all kinds of cakes and breads in store."

"We sell all kinds of cars, all models."

"We have different packages meeting different pricing needs."

The examples above are product-focused, which is the same as saying "company-focused." You want your website to be solution-focused, which is the same as "customer-focused."

Gifts and Bonuses

You should always have something free to offer for your clients. In exchange for this free service, you should ask for their feedback or their email address. In today's business model, free has to be incorporated in all your services and products. This is how you get to test your product or your service and get free marketing through your customers.

Remember, your clients may not buy your premium product or service today or tomorrow, but if they like your product and service, if they like the value your product and services add to their lives, they will most certainly buy them when they can afford it. They will most certainly recommend them to their friends and family.

Case Studies

Offer case studies on your website. Case studies can be made available for download or physically sent out to a postal address. Case studies of your products and services highlighting their importance in the market niche together with the benefits and solutions your company provides will help potential customers become customers. Case studies also:

122

- Call attention to existing problems in the market.

- Create an awareness of what harm these existing problems can cause.

- Showcase the emotional and economic benefits your service and products provide to the end-user.

Having case studies available for download on your website establishes you as an industry expert. Offer the case studies for free download, but in return ask for the recipient's email address or postal address. Seek a connection to which you can go back for sending out newsletters or sending out marketing emails. You have to offer something for free to get something in return.

The First Ten Seconds

Your website is the first point of entry for most of your clients. You should be curious to know what the link was about when they clicked. You have ten seconds to impress them. What are you going to have on your front page that will convey your brand, your cause, your products, your solutions and your company in ten seconds?

I believe that by connecting emotionally with the reader you will increase your chances of them staying on your website longer and referring it to another friend. The only way to connect emotionally with your potential client is by highlighting the problem they are facing.

In ten seconds, they will read a single line or three lines because an average human mind can only read about twenty to thirty words in ten seconds and be able to decide if that content is helpful or a waste of time. You need to ensure the content in the top part of your website homepage is all about

123

your end-user and their problems. This is needed to get their attention. Once you have it, you can then talk about your company and your products and your deals.

People want to know about you and your company before they consider buying your product or even looking into your products page. In the "about us" page, you need to advertise your values and vision. They don't want to know who is running the company and they don't want to know who the director, CEO or your team are. They don't want to know when it was established. This is valid information to put on the about us page, but that is not the killing factor for getting a client. This is the place to mention the charities you support and to talk about your working culture and how your company runs.

In the about us page, you talk about your vision what you want to achieve by bringing this product and service into the market. You need to add your values, the core values that you stand by and work with. When you add values and vision, and if the values and vision of your company resonate with the reader, then you have already established an emotional connection. When an emotional connection is established, the next thing the reader wants to know is how you are implementing the values and vision in your products and services.

The user will then navigate to the services page or products page. Once the user is on the services and products page, you have another task: highlighting the emotional connection about the end-user with your service and product. You highlight the common problems, you highlight the common gaps in the market, you highlight the coolness in terms of style and behaviour that your service or product represents and how it will benefit the end-user. You do not talk about products.

Infographics

Infographics are a new and most effective way to convey lots of data and lots of words within a short span of time and succinctly to your site visitor.

On your website, you might also want to consider having infographics in addition to text. You can create infographics for free by using tools available online. In these infographics, you can showcase your services and solutions as a positive emotional value. Showcase clients happy and energetic and feeling emotionally alive after using your products and services. Infographics like these play a huge part in your marketing. You have to accept the fact that you clients are people and people absorb information in different media types. Certain people absorb information differently when presented using a different media type, so you'll have to cater to all types of people. This might have been an expensive exercise before, but now the fact that you can create an infographic document for your service and product for free by using the tools available online means you can and should get it done today, now.

Free Infographic tools

- Vizualize.me
- Infogr.am
- iCharts
- Piktochart

Online Tools to Create Infographics

125

The 3+ Door Knock Sale Technique

One way to increase sales is by having a 3+ Door Knock sale technique. This system has an advantage over the basic system where a sale is attempted on a basic yes/no logic. The outcome is either "yes, I will buy your product" or "no thank you, I will not buy your product."

Free	Basic	Medium	Premium
• Something free • A taster session of your product	• With 2-3 features • Eg:The Curious	• With 5-6 features • Eg:The Brave	• All the features • Eg: The Adventourous

3+ Door Knock Sale techniques

The 3+ Door Knock Sale techniques will give you an advantage of having different products and services highlighted in three different buckets. Having this approach gives the user more options to consider for the same product, yet gives the user an option to choose what type of level of service the user would like to choose.

Four-Step Sale Approach

Here is a simple four-step sale approach which you must ensure is being followed by your marketing or sales team and by yourself:

- Build a relationship with your potential client.
- Identify their problems.
- Provide a solution and a product or service.

126

- Follow-up after the sale to make sure they are satisfied and build a client relationship.

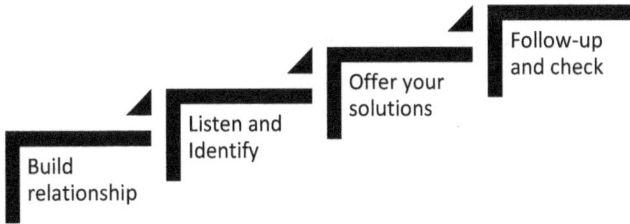

4-Step Sale approach

Rise of the New Hyper-individual

Today's customer is more active on-line and has evolved into a "hyper-individual." Your customer has more access to information in the palms of their hands – via smart devices – than ever before.

How does the hyper-individual shop?

- Check if there are similar products in the industry.
- Compare price and services.
- Read reviews from other customers.
- Check for reviews from industry experts.
- Share products on their social accounts to ask their friends for their opinions.

You website must have client testimonials, plugins to enable sharing of your content across different social accounts and blog articles talking about the values your products have.

127

Blog Your Way to Success

Having a blog increases the chances of getting more visitors to your website. When you add appropriate articles about your solutions and values, the content will immediately connect with the reader, thus leading them your main website. You need to share articles using your social media tools.

I recommend you reading a great book, *How to TurboCharge your business with a BLOG* for more information about blogging.

Sample blog titles might be:

- 5 Common mistakes customers do when choosing (a product).
- 3 steps to easily achieve ………..(your solutions)
- 10 tips to enhance your current situation on ………….. (Problems your product solves).

Know Your Visitors

It is important to know how your site visitors are interacting with your content. Google Analytics provides very powerful statistics about your site visitors.

Let's say Mary is a visitor who has landed on your site and is browsing. Using Google Analytics, you can find out:

- Which part of the world is Mary from?
- How did she find out about my site?
- Which page did Mary visit?

128

Use Google Analytics to:

- Track how many visitors are on your site in real time.
- Track the key words by which they got to your site.
- Track the visitor's location and language.
- Track how many new and returning visitors are coming to your site.
- Track patterns in how your visitors navigate around on your site.
- Track from which page your visitor exits your site.

The above points are only a simple overview of how Google Analytics can help you understand your site traffic and your visitors.

Getting your website working the way you want may take time. Be patient, but strive for constant improvement.

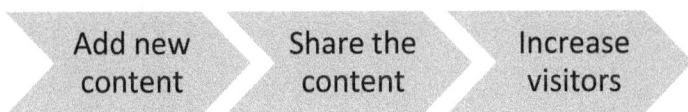

Add new content	Share the content	Increase visitors

3 actions to increase buyers on your website

130

Chapter 12

Worried About Competition

Competition is such a virtue, and everybody's so busy competing, they forget to serve their clients. – Major Owens[12]

You can't focus both on your customers and on your competition if you want to succeed. You may gain customers by trying to win them on price, but this will lead you to start compromising the quality of your products and eventually on the quality of customer service.

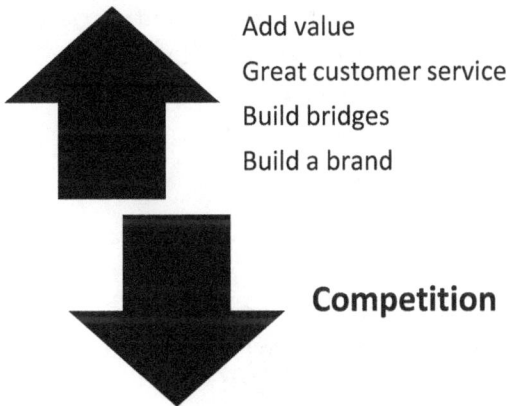

Add value
Great customer service
Build bridges
Build a brand

Competition

4 ways to vanquish competition

---

[12] Major Owens – New York politician and prominent member of Democratic Party

The Unique SMART Analysis™

SMART™ Steps Lead to Longer Strides

The difference between ordinary and extraordinary is the "extra." Empower your front line staff with extra resources they can use to transform your clients' experience from something ordinary to something amazing.

For example, here's a process Peter Sage uses in many of his companies, one of which happen to be a gym. Peter has empowered his front line team behind the reception with a £ 50 note. The employees are allowed to use that resource to transform a customer's average gym experience into an amazing experience.

One day, a customer walked into their gym talking to a friend on phone. He mentioned to his friend that his car tyre got punctured while driving into the gym car park. One of the employees heard this conversation, took the £ 50 note and called a local garage to come and fix the customer's car tyre. When the customer finished his workout and was on the way out of the gym, one of the employees handed him a note which said, "Sorry, it must have been a nail in our car park. Your car tyre is now fixed."

This is an extra which makes the customer service go an extra mile. This is marketing free of charge. Your customer is the cheapest and the most effective marketing you can get. You can convert any customer into a loyal customer for life by simply being a customer-oriented business.

A merchant who approaches business with the idea of serving the public well has nothing to fear from the competition. – James Cash Penney[13]

Lead the Way

As the CEO and founder of your company, you will be tied down with many important decision making tasks which will demand your highest concentration and focus to ensure the best decision is made. Nevertheless, it is important that you dedicate time off from your busy schedule and focus it on your customers. The reason you are so busy is because of your customers, so it is important that you set some time aside and address them directly to elevate their customer service experience. SMART advocates companies to provide quality customer service to achieve great success. You need to know your customers and connect with your customers.

Great CEOs do this. And this is the difference between being a multinational company and a success and any other small business or start-up which doesn't get to celebrate their third or fifth anniversary because they're already closed down or into administration.

The CEO of 4G mobile network EE calls five customers every day, first thing in the morning, to find out how their network is doing. This is customer service at the highest levels. By doing this, you are not only making your customer feel special; you are also your also seeding potential marketing agents into them. They will talk to friends and family about the telephone conversation they had with a CEO. That's branding, customer service and adding value to your customers and clients.

---

[13] J.C.Penny – American businessman and entrepreneur who, in 1902, founded the J.C.Penny stores.

What If There Is Already a Competitor?

Being second in the market is sometimes good because you already know your target clients and their expectations. You can model your services and solutions by addressing the gap which is left by your competitors. If the competitor or competitors are not addressing a key emotional requirement of their clients, then you being a follower have an advantage of incorporating that emotional aspect into your service and products. The best example is Apple. Apple was not the first in the market for bringing out portable music players. Apple was not the first to bring out touch screen phones, nor were they first in introducing a tablet. Having said that, they were very particular about what emotional attribute they wanted to add to the existing market. They applied it with meticulous research and design. Applying this attitude towards competition will give you a great advantage over your competitors.

My Competitor Is Very Big and Very Well Established

Do not worry about the big players. All you have to focus on is being yourself and applying your personal attitude and characteristics to your service and product. Apple achieved greater success because they did exactly the same thing. Their micro-niche was their ability to be perfect and meticulous when it came to designing their products. Their micro-niche was to enhance the end-user's interaction with the product. They introduced a new emotional necessity in the market. They focused only on themselves and did not worry about Samsung, Sony, Ericsson and Nokia. Nokia was the world leader at that time and Apple wiped them out. So identify what micro-niche you can introduce to the market that will make your product stand out.

134

Evolve Your Brand, but Don't Change It

One of the important aspects of SMART™ is being agile. Agility is being flexible, being aware of your market and having the attitude to incorporate change and finding a balance in maintaining your brand values.

To emphasise my point of being agile, I would like to talk about Skype and Hotmail. The founders of Skype initially built Kazaa, which is a peer-to-peer file sharing application. Having realised their potential and analysing the market need of the day by looking out for trends, they then went on and developed Skype. Skype now is a platform for people to communicate all over the world.

At Hotmail, Sameer Bhatia and Jack Smith initially wanted to build a personal database system for the end-user to store their data and be able to access it. In that process, the two founders found it very hard to communicate with each other while one of them was working in a full employment job. To solve the difficulty, they devised a method by which they could communicate with each other through a browser. This was how Hotmail was born.

Being agile is having that mind-set where you are constantly absorbing the information and turn of events happening around you and seeing how you can apply them to your business model and transform them into another package or another service. If Skype and Hotmail had been complacent, they would have never come up with the applications that have transformed today's communication market.

135

Build Bridges

One of the best ways to surpass the hurdle of competition is to remove it and replace it with a bridge. Partnerships have a great potential to grow your company into a global brand. The moment you work with other companies through collaboration and affiliation, you will build a great network of likeminded people. This bridge does not have to be restricted locally or nationally; you can go global and find partners in other parts of the world. Take advantage of today's technological marvels which provide you the tools of collaboration even when both parties are thousands of miles apart.

Competition has been shown to be useful up to a certain point and no further, but cooperation, which is the thing we must strive for today, begins where competition leaves off.– Franklin D. Roosevelt[14]

---

14 Franklin D. Roosevelt – 32nd President of the United States of America

The Unique SMART Analysis™

Chapter 13

Marketing Is a Bitch

Marketing is an essential part of any business. You need to advertise that you are in business. It is important you let your potential clients be aware of your services and products. You need to devote time and resources aside from your business to achieve the art of marketing, nevertheless, devoting too much to this endeavour can also work against you.

It is not what you say but how you say it that distinguishes you from rest of the market.

You have been so lucky to have chosen to do business in this era of information and technology, one in which you are empowered with amazing and effective marketing tools for both online and off-line. The Unique SMART Analysis™ has laid down some simple and effective marketing strategies for you to succeed in your business.

The Three Great Marketeers

Off-line: You need to network with people in person. It is important that you meet and greet because this adds a personal touch to the company.

- **Give something free**: You have to offer something free for your potential customers. This can be a simple version of your product which will have all the basic deliverables in it.

137

- **Press releases**: Create a press release about your company, your services and products and send it to newspapers and magazines which are focused in your area of expertise.

- **Responsible marketing**: Sponsor a club or a sports team. This team can be from your local school or local area. It can be a football team, chess team or electronics club. Wouldn't it be great to have your company's logo on the team's T-shirts and equipment? Also see if you can give away some of your products and services as prizes when your supported team is playing at home. If you choose to support a club, then have free products to give away for the best contributor or dedicated member of the club.

- **Network with people**: Take time off your work to go and meet likeminded people. Build a nice, friendly relationship with people who you feel understand your vision and what your company does. The other person does not have to be from the same industry. You are not looking for people who admire your products and services in these networking events; you are looking for people who admire your company's vision, your company's working culture and your company's effort to support a charity and cause. Find a handful of people in every meet and invest time in building the relationship later after the meet. If you are very busy and cannot attend then find people within your own company who like to meet new people. Send them to local Meetup.com group meets and networking events.

Along with the above important SMART Analysis™ techniques, you also need to have the elementary marketing kit for your company, like:

- Business cards
- Flyers
- Big banners
- A company flag

Online: To take advantage of your online presence and the way social platforms have spread in the last three years, you need to have online marketing strategies as well.

- **Social presence**: Maintaining a social presence on platforms like Facebook, Google+, Twitter and LinkedIn is important. Having said that, the most crucial point missed by many companies having a social presence is having only one account across all platforms. This can get confusing for the people. Sometimes they might get irritated and frustrated looking at your tweets and posts about your products and services, your solutions and your offers; having posts about all of them in the same platform can have a negative effect on your company. You stand the risk of losing valuable customers. SMART Analysis™ believes that the solution to this is having separate social accounts with each having a consistent pattern in its information. For example you can have separate accounts for:
    - o Talking about company values, vision and culture.
    - o Talking about your solutions and services. Here you can also include offers and

139

information about some of your free products and services.

- o One for the CEO, who talks about his vision for his company, his clients and what steps his company is taking to change the world by supporting charities and causes around the world.

- **Emails:** This type of marketing works only if you honour and respect your recipients' privacy. *Never share your lists with other parties.* With online platforms like MailChimp, you can very easily set up processes that will automatically send emails to your subscribers. Again, the trick is to pace it out and not bombard your recipients with multiple emails in a week. You also have to pay close attention to how you manage your list of emails; you cannot mix and match your lists. E.g. when a customer signs up for free information about a certain service after reading one of your blog posts, you need to only send information of new blog posts and other related posts; you cannot start emailing them about your products and offers. You can, however, ask them in your emails if they are interested in subscribing to your other mails where in which you talk about your solutions and occasionally give away free stuff. Let the recipient decide if they want to get on a different list.

- **Webinars and hangouts:** With the latest improvements in online networking, you can hold free webinars on Google+. Hold them periodically and maintain the consistency of the format in which you conduct them. To start off with, you can always have

140

shorter versions of webinars and hangouts. The important point to note is that you need to follow a strict schedule; you can even send out a monthly or half-yearly schedule for these sessions. This is a great way to engage your existing clients and attract new clients. The most common mistake made in these webinars is talking about your company, your latest offers and products. This can turn off your audience. Yes, you are dedicating your time and resources to market your services and solutions, but if you talk about yourself first all the time you will lose the focus of your listeners and viewers. Find a balance in talking about quality content and your products

Industry: The third and the most important part of your marketing is your presence in the industry. Whichever market or industry your services are targeting, you need to attend and make your company's presence felt in conferences. They may be several conferences hosted; you may pick and choose whichever depending on the location, topic and registration fees. You need to start off by having your company's presence felt in these conferences at least once a year. If possible, you must also encourage your team members or your employees to go as well. These activities help brand your company to the outside world.

I love attending industry conferences alongside my business; because this is what I love; I make time and find energy to attend these events. My next event will be IS&T SPIE conference in February 3-7, 2013 at California – Dr.Nagachetan

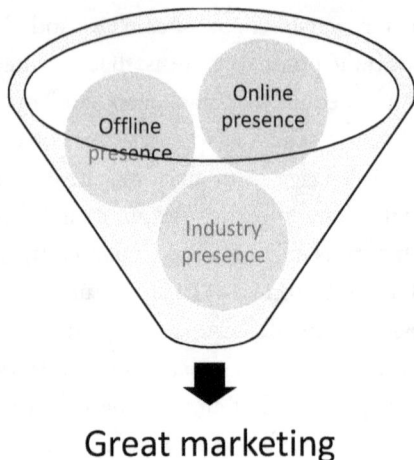

Great marketing

The 3 great marketeers

Customer Service Is Excellent Marketing

Customer service is everything. It is the cheapest form of marketing a company can get. If you're spending thousands of pounds in marketing at the moment, rethink. Re-purpose that budget for marketing into providing excellent customer service. Providing excellent customer service will give you free marketing. Why? When you provide excellent customer service, your client will talk about the positive experience they had with you to ten more people. Marketing is all about sharing your brand to more people and convincing them that you are adding value. And satisfied customers are happy to do this at no cost to you.

Send business seasonal cards, birthday cards and festival cards to your clients as part of your follow-up sales approach. Let them know that you are a people company and not driven by sales and numbers. Mention your company's name and logo or

142

brand in a very subtle manner. This card must resemble a normal card and not be too branded about your products and services. If it is too branded, the person might not be interested to display it. However, if the product and brand logo is present only on the back of the card then your customer will proudly showcase your card and display it to their friends and family. Again, the importance of great customer service relationships is having free marketing and an extended marketing team.

Know your client. Know what type of people usually buy a product of yours and which part of the world would you like to target. Knowing this information will help your marketing team and your sales team to have more clarity to manage your resources and channel the information in the right direction to the right people and, most importantly, using the right methods.

Always aim for quality – Chaulas

I create a circumstance right in front of their eyes where they immediately feel the need for it by the value my product adds to their lives – Nagachetan

Advertise in Online Supermarkets

The supermarkets we know are the big malls at the centre of the city which house all the top brands in the industry. People come to these super markets to buy items they like and in most cases they come and buy items they do not like as well. Supermarkets are great for sales. As a small business owner you might be thinking, "Hey, SMART™ guy, I cannot afford to rent a shop in one of those high street supermarkets. Tell me

143

something I *can* do." I get it, and SMART Analysis™ techniques are made for small businesses. Some of them are:

- If you are service provider then list your company on Elance. This is a great way to harness small clients which may lead to bigger contracts.

- Advertise your products on ClickBank. This is the online wholesale department store. Here, retailers from across the world come and search for products they can sell by setting up an affiliate link you with you product. They then go about and start spreading that link in your industry-specific forums and blogs. When you list your products here, you will attract online retailers selling your products for you. You will have to give a small bit of commission, but isn't it great that your products will get worldwide coverage? It is better when you are initially growing and want people to visit your site so that they can get to know more about your company and the solutions you offer.

Chapter 14

Time to Take Action

SMART™ Techniques

This chapter is all about implementing the Unique SMART Analysis™ techniques.

The techniques below can be used by both entrepreneurs and small businesses. You can jump straight to the relevant section and start implementing new techniques all by yourself or contact The Unique SMART Analysis™ by going to our website, *www.thesmartanalysis.com,* and getting help from professionals.

In each section, Unique SMART Analysis™ has laid down an effective process path. You can jump straight to a process which suits you or follow the entire path from beginning to end for success.

Entrepreneur and a BRAND New Idea

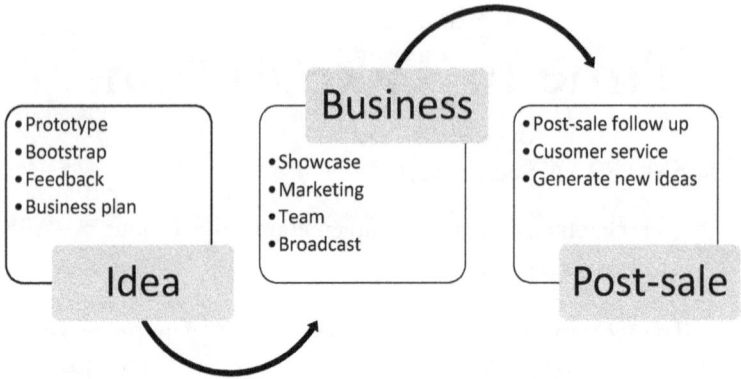

The idea-to-customer feedback

IDEA: The Big BRAND Theory

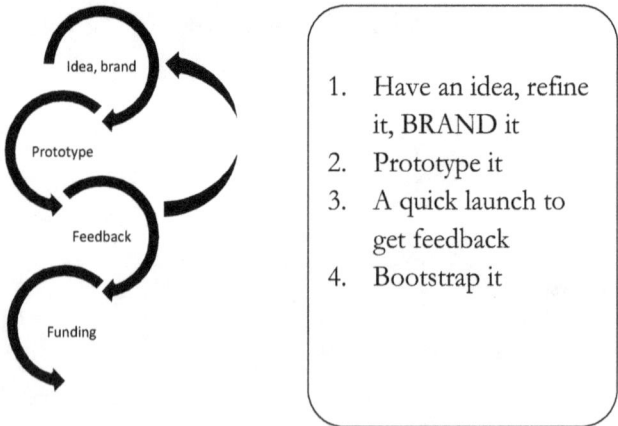

1. Have an idea, refine it, BRAND it
2. Prototype it
3. A quick launch to get feedback
4. Bootstrap it

4 steps to make your idea a success

146

In this stage, you refine your ideas and start a brand.

- What will my brand be?
- What are the current problems faced by customers?
- What is my niche? (i.e. my uniqueness, the thing I love doing)
- Which market will my idea best suit?
- Are there any products which resemble my idea already?
- Who will benefit from my idea?
- What will my business vision be?

In this stage, you prototype your ideas into a commodity.

- What is the quickest way I can implement this idea? (- choose freely available resources)
- How can I bootstrap this?
- What is my brand name?

The Unique SMART Analysis™

In this stage, you create a business plan.

You need 3 types of business plan.
1. Mini plan
    o   5-7 pages long
    o   To attract initial partners and team members
    o   To present to investors
2. Working plan
    o   This is for internal use only
    o   List all the operational processes
    o   All available resources and roles of team members. This will be useful when deciding to delegate and outsource.
    o   Who will do which processes?
3. Presentation plan
    o   This is to show to bankers, capitalists and investors
    o   Must be able to present in 20 minutes and with 10 slides ONLY
    o   Lots of images, charts

Business plan must include:

*   Your plan must be simple, easy to read and have consistent formatting
*   Your company name, brand, vision, products and services
*   Your target market and your ideal customer
*   Your micro-niche: what makes you different from others
*   Your contact details
*   Your required initial start-up funds
*   Operations involved to deliver your products and services
*   Your company culture & reward system to attract the ideal team; the charities your company supports
*   Your marketing strategy
*   Your customer service strategy
*   Your cash flow management and financial projections
*   Your growth strategy and quarterly targets
*   Your exit strategy

In this stage, you fund your project on a small scale.

- Borrow from family and friends
- For resources, use the barter system
- Go for all the free tools available online and offline
  - Websites : Weebly, Google Sites
  - Local listings like Friday Ads, Craigslist
- Start small with small money
-

In this stage, you seek funding to start.

- Seeking for funding from banks
- Seeking for funding from VC and investors by meeting them at your local Meetup groups and other arenas
- Seek public help to fund from places like KickStarter.com

BUSINESS: It's about Your BRAND

Showcase
- Services and solutions
- Supporting charities
- A website
- 3+ Door Knock Sales

Broadcast
- Social media
- Local groups
- Marketing
- A blog
- A forum

Team
- Roles and responsibilities
- Delegate tasks
- Outsource
- Rewarding team

3 Tier business elements

In this stage, you broadcast your solutions and values.

Website

Your website is your premium online estate. It is your retail shop or advertisement billboard on the information highway. You have to keep your message simple, clear and consistent.

Ingredients for a website:

1. **Domain name:** This is your web address, like Google.com and thesmartanalysis.com and runbeforeyouwalkbook.com. Once you have decided on the name of your **BRAND** and your company name, you can go about and purchase your domain. Always go for a .com domain. Be creative if your name is not available. Your domain name does not have to be the name of your company. Get your domain name from:
   a. 1and1 services
   b. GoDaddy
2. **Hosting services:** A place to host your website. If the domain name is your address, then you need a plot to house your building. You can choose between Windows and Linux platforms. Once you know what kind of website you want to build then you will be able to choose from Linux or Windows.
   a. 1and1 services
   b. GoDaddy
3. **Website:** The sky is your limit when it comes to building a website. To start off I would recommend **WordPress** because it is widely used and has an established community from which you can learn a lot and get help from. All of the hosting services can support a WordPress site.

Important: Brand, logo, description must be consistent with your social media accounts.

150

Blogging

Your website is not complete until it has a blog. Your business needs a blog to interact with your customers. You have more chances of converting a potential customer into a paid customer by having an article. It also makes your website dynamic and alive rather than static text added at the time it was published.

Samples articles:

- 5 values added by your product
- 3 problems currently faced by customers
- 5 solutions we offer for each problem
- About your vision and goals
- List the charities you donate to and support
- Create a mobile application for your business
  - Application is your free marketing tool
  - Use BuzzTouch.com to design your application

Mobile Presence

In light of the latest trend in the market where everybody has a smart device, you need to be present on their devices as well. Having a free standalone application about your brand, about your values and solutions will give you a better chance of getting new customers.

A free application can be built using BuzzTouch.com. With BuzzTouch, you can easily build an application with no coding experience. You might need a developer to help you get the application onto market.

Application features can be simple:

- Your brand, your values your solutions
- RSS feeds from your social media platforms
- News about your company
- Your latest blog articles

151

Social Media and News

Your brand must be present on all the major social media platforms. This will enable you to reach out to far greater audience.

- Open social accounts for business on all major platforms
  - o   Facebook page
  - o   Google+ page
  - o   Twitter accounts
  - o   LinkedIn account for your company
  - o   Showcase your products on Pinterest.com
- Meet new potential customers at local meets and conferences
  - o   Search on MeetUp.com to find your group
  - o   Setup an account on getlunched.com and build bridges
- Send out press releases online using
  - o   Contact your local newspapers
  - o   Use online services like: 24-7PressPrelease.com, I-Newswire.com and PRBuzz.com.
  - o   Have your own online newspaper using services from Paper.li

"Managing so many social accounts is driving me mad."

1. Search for HootSuite on Google and open their site
2. Open a free account by filling in the registration instructions
3. For free you can attach up to 5 of your social media accounts
4. You can save your commonly used posts as drafts
5. You can schedule a post in advance
6. You get to choose which accounts you want to share separately
7. The pro version has lot more features; upgrade if you feel the need to

There are similar online tools like – Tweetdeck, Buffer and SocialOomph but HootSuite is my favourite.

152

In this stage, you start selling and make money!

- Go live, set up a shop or a website to pull in customers
- Use the **3+ Door Knock Sales** technique to sell
- Give something free to attract your clients onto premium products
- Phase your release to smaller groups so that you can get feedback
  - Invites only
  - First 100 or 500

3+ Door Knock Sales Technique

Have something **FREE** to offer to your first time customers.
1. **Basic:** Slimmed down version of your products or services. E.g.: $25/month
2. **Medium:** Add more features and services to this knock E.g.: $75/month
3. **Premium:** All the features, services, 24/7 support; this should be the best quality service and product. E.g.,: $150/month

Free	Basic	Medium	Premium
• Something free • A taster session of your product	• With 2-3 features • Eg:The Curious	• With 5-6 features • Eg:The Brave	• All the features • Eg: The Adventourous

3+ Door Knock Sale techniques

153

In this stage, you risk getting pulled into all sorts of work.

When you go live, you will be overwhelmed with response and tasks that you will have to do in-order to keep up with your customers to ensure quality service. It is important you anticipate them beforehand and have measures to potentially delegate and outsource.

- **IMPORTANT**: You need to know everything there is about your business
- **IMPORTANT**: You need to know what processes are involved
- **IMPORTANT**: You need to know the cost and time involved in each process
- **VERY IMPORTANT**: Once you know everything there is about a certain process, OUTSOURCE or DELEGATE to experts
- Prioritise all your tasks into
  - o Immediate: Can be done today with ROI huge
  - o Moderate: Can be done in a week
  - o Normal: Can be done in a month

POST-SALE: Follow Your BRAND and Grow It

In this stage, you follow up with customers for feedback.

Sale Follow-up

This is the most important part of business. 70% of businesses fail to do this right; shockingly 90% of businesses don't even do this.

The main objective of this process is to verify whether your products and services have delivered its intended purpose.

- Has your product enriched your clients?
- Have your product and services solved their problems?
- What values has it added to your customer's life?

This information can be obtained by both on-line and off-line media

Online

Send follow-up emails to check their feedback. These emails have to be sent out using a professional email management service like MailChimp (my preference). Every email must:

- Mention of your brand
- Be consistent
- Be sent at regular intervals
- Be not more than 2 a month in numbers
- Not be about sales and marketing
- Email addresses must be kept **confidential** at all times

Off-line

- Meet your customers in person if possible
- Call your customers to check how they are doing with your products and services. To make a difference, as the CEO / founder of your business you call them in person

155

In this stage, you create an ecosystem for your customers.

An Ecosystem for Your Clients

Have a large vision for your brand. Build an ecosystem for your customers around your services and products.

- A forum for them to interact and request new features
- Training modules on how to make the best use of your products and services
- Hold regular webinars by inviting an industry expert
- Host an evening party for your customers, an excellent chance for them to meet your team.

In this stage, you get information you'll need to build your next product.

A Nursery for New Ideas

Use crowd-sourcing to gather invaluable feedback data from clients and use them to:

- Enhance the features of the current product and services
- Create and innovate new products
- See if your products now can be repackaged to another market

Caution: The above techniques are not suitable for entrepreneurs who are allergic to success and business growth.

156

Feel free to follow above SMART Analysis™ in the same order as prescribed or jump straight to a technique and start implementing the SMART Analysis™ techniques.

Two ways to implement the above techniques into your business or idea:

1. By yourself.
2. Go to *www.thesmartanalysis.com* and contact professional help who will implement all of the above techniques for you.

The Unique SMART Analysis™

The Unique SMART Analysis™

Chapter 15

Inspirational CEOs and Entrepreneurs

VISIO INGENII

Dr. Nagachetan Bangalore
CEO and co-founder

Visio Ingenii means "vision intelligence" in Latin. VI was born with a passion to introduce the next-generation machine-vision-based technology solutions to the defence, security, transportation, medical and retail industries. The chief objective of VI is to improve security and safety by making intelligence more powerful than ever and, most importantly, make it more relevant and timely.

Dr. Bangalore is one of the few people on the planet who has mastered the art of converting conceptual research work into a high-value product for the consumer. Nagachetan has published several publications and contributed to the computer vision industry. His areas of interest include but are not limited to: scientific research, operations, strategic planning, human resources, risk management, quality assurance, and information systems, general and administrative tasks.

159

FrontPoint Systems

Arun Shroff

Entrepreneur, Advisor, Technology Consulting

Arun is an entrepreneur and the founder/co-founder of several web and technology companies and websites, some of which are:

- **FrontPoint Systems**: Managed web hosting, web applications.
- **Medindia.net**: India's #1 health website - over 5 million page views/month.
- **Medwonders.com**: A social network for health professionals
- **India4u.com**: One of the earliest websites on India.
- **Dynapro**: The first tech company started in India back in early 90's. A VAR and systems integrator.
- **Pcportable.com**: An early e-commerce company that sold customized portable computers via the web.

Having founded and managed several web and technology companies, he is also a mentor and an advisor who provides management and technology consulting services to both start-ups and established businesses and helps them grow and succeed.

Arun is also a responsible entrepreneur who takes time out of his busy schedule and support several charities and global causes like human rights, global health and poverty alleviation.

Marketing Fundamentals, Ltd

Mike Pitt

CEO and founder

Before starting Marketing Fundamentals, Mike worked with global businesses such as Coca-Cola, Hewlett Packard, Wilkinson Sword, Prudential and Vauxhall.

Through Marketing Fundamentals, he has worked with several SMEs, entrepreneurs and business start-ups and helped them turbocharge their business by having a blog. His specializes in giving them marketing expertise at a time when they most need it. The scope of his work for Marketing Fundamentals, Ltd is varied, but the primary focus is content marketing, specifically blogging.

His latest book, *How to TurboCharge Your Business with a BLOG*, is a practical guide for business owners and entrepreneurs for creating a successful blog.

Chaula's

Chaula Patel

Business Owner

Chaula is a self-made businesswoman with a passion for cooking tasty Indian curry. She has built a chain of restaurants in East Sussex, UK. She started selling her curries at her local newsagent store and built a great brand. Her vision is to serve great Indian dishes by showing the world how spicy food and great cooking come together in an enjoyable dish.

161

About the Author

Chinmai Swamy lives in Brighton, UK with his lovely wife. He is passionate, adventurous and a risk taker. This book is inspired by his experience gained by working for global giants to small businesses. An entrepreneur at heart, he started his own PC solutions business when he was still at college. The book reflects some of the confidence gained through achievements such as a black belt in Karate, a national medal in rowing and his Himalayan mountaineering adventures which have taught him to view life with humility, desire to help those in need and to strive for excellence with a ceaseless passion.

Chinmai Swamy

CEO and Founder of The SMART Analysis Ltd

www.chinmaiswamy.com

www.thesmartanalysis.com

www.ismallbusinessbranding.com

Thank you for reading

www.ingramcontent.com/pod-product-compliance
Lightning Source LLC
Chambersburg PA
CBHW031959190326
41520CB00007B/300